The New England
MARINER
TRADITION

The New England MARINER TRADITION

OLD SALTS, SUPERSTITIONS, SHANTIES & SHIPWRECKS

ROBERT A. GEAKE

Charleston · London

THE
History
PRESS

Published by The History Press
Charleston, SC 29403
www.historypress.net

Copyright © 2013 by Robert A. Geake
All rights reserved

First published 2013

Manufactured in the United States

ISBN 978.1.62619.228.7

Library of Congress CIP data applied for.

This book is dedicated to the memory of my ancestor First Mate Nicholas Easton, originally from Newport, who was lost at sea in 1828 off the Cape of Good Hope while aboard the whaling ship Zone, *at the age of thirty-two.*

Contents

Acknowledgements

Impacable I, the old implacable Sea:
implacable most when I smile serene-
Pleased, not appeased by myriad wrecks in me
—Herman Melville, "Pebbles"

My efforts to understand the adventures and lives of the mariners of New England began with reading Melville. Not with the momentous *Moby Dick*, as you may already have surmised, but with the lesser work *White Jacket*, which gave a glimpse into life on an American naval ship in the early nineteenth century. It was a rigid, confining and often violent world these sailors lived in, and it prepared me for reading *Moby Dick* the following year. I wallowed slowly through the book like the proverbial drunken sailor, utterly intoxicated by the story and the world that was presented to me at fourteen. Even though I was reading Melville's masterpiece 120 years after its publication, living in New England with the ocean and the historical architecture from that era all around, I felt a distinct connection to his story.

As an adult, I've continued learning of the mariner's life, mainly from reading those historians mentioned throughout this book. Anyone wanting to learn more of New England's mariners should reference the bibliography, where those historians to whom I am indebted, and their books, are duly noted.

I want to thank the staff of the John Carter Brown Library for their assistance in finding needed books and materials, as well as the staff of the John Hay Library for their assistance in navigating their fine Whaling Collection. Thanks must also go to Henry A.L. Brown for his astonishing collection of Rhode Island ephemera as well as his personal knowledge of Rhode Island's shoreline and the lifesaving stations of the coast. The New Bedford Whaling Museum and Library were helpful in providing both physical and digital logbooks for my research, and the Special Collections Department of the Providence Public Library, which has an unparalleled collection of whaling logbooks, records and memorabilia in the state, is a valuable resource for any researcher.

Introduction

In the winter of 1779–80, young merchant seaman Charles Carroll, working on his father's ship, the *Family Trader*, on a voyage to Guadalupe, recorded in his journal that on December 2, 1779, "Mr. Tropic Man paid us a visit in a very frightful dress. Had a demand of Mr. Taylor passenger of whom he received a case bottle gin."

On the ship's return voyage to South Carolina a month later, Carroll and the crew found themselves in the path of another squall. On January 7, 1780, he recorded, "Today also, the wind very Hard with Seas mountain High…a Consultation held to Conclude Whether we should beat about Here…or to return to the West Indies for water and provisions. It was unanimously agreed to Waite here…to see what the Almighty would decree…Kept Centry in the cabin tonight as we were very suspicious of 6 or 7 in our crews rising and taking the vessel or at Least doing a deal of mischief."[1]

These two passages highlight only a small part of what any seaman working on naval, merchant, whaling, privateering or slaving ships faced on each voyage into the Atlantic and beyond. During any cruise, potentially fatal storms, low provisions, disease, violence among the crew and the practice of old superstitions, such as the offering of "a case bottle gin" to appease Neptune and save the ship and crew, could be expected to be encountered. Many were the causes of death at sea.

In this book, I want to explore the preparations seamen made for voyages with their own mortality in mind, the rituals practiced onboard for the crew's safety and those after tragedy struck and the remembrance of these captains and crew members onboard ship and at home in their various forms. In this way, I hope to touch on some forgotten traditions among these mariners in the age of sail and to recover, as well, a glimpse into their lives on the sea and at home, where family members waited for their return.

By the end of the seventeenth century, there had been a long-established brotherhood among seamen of many races in the Atlantic trade. The journal of Edward Barlow, the son of an English farmer whose descriptions and accounts of life at sea cover over forty years of voyages, gives such a glimpse into these early practices and presents a stark truth of circumstance that would prove to be the great factor in the gathering of crews from the port cities of both England and the Colonies. He writes, "In the later end of April in the year 1675, I began to prepare myself for another voyage to sea, for my money would not hold out...and having no other calling but the sea to get my livelihood by, I must go, yet I wished many times that I had a trade, so that I may have got my living ashore when I had been weary of the sea, but for that I had nobody to blame but my own foolish fancy."[2]

Marcus Rediker wrote that the "high mortality rate and the rigors of maritime work made seafaring a young man's occupation and culture," and while it was true, as the historian concluded, that most seamen were between twenty and forty years of age, some, like Barlow, were destined to become "old salts."

Barlow saw this life ahead as "a great grief for an aged man" and wrote gloomily of the fate he saw for himself and others, "to be little more than a slave, being always in need, and enduring all manner of misery and hardship, going with many a hungry belly and wet back."

Of course, longevity was a rarity among seamen, "for they seldom live until they be old," Barlow wrote. "They either die with want or with grief to see themselves so little regarded."

Life at sea for the ordinary and able-bodied seamen was an extreme hardship, and while much was made of the toughness of "Jack Tar" in the lore and literature that appeared during the age of sail, these sons, husbands and fathers who toiled aboard ships left remarkable legacies of love of family in letters, in song and in poignant scenes scrimshawed on ivory. They lived and worked always under the dark cloud of knowing that death could come at any moment.

Rediker would write that, "As callous as the seaman appeared toward the death that took many shapes around him, he could not escape its shadows."[3]

A scrimshaw portrait of a thankful sailor returned home. *From the collection of the New Bedford Whaling Museum.*

Those same shadows gathered for those at home whose loved ones were at sea. Reminders of death were in every seaside village, with their cemetery rows of grinning skulls on every stone. The stories of lost sailors were often chiseled out on a monument above an empty grave, and always, there was the mournful repetition of the tide crashing ashore and withdrawing again, to remind those left behind of the peril.

In prayers, hymns and poetry, the plea for a sailor's safety was intoned to the Almighty, and these same mediums were employed, along with others, when these pleas went unanswered, and word of a tragedy reached home.

I began researching this book by looking at those remnants of tragedies: the tombstones in the oldest cemetery in Newport, Rhode Island, and the songs, poems and broadsheets that memorialized those lost at sea. Like many others, I wanted to know what their lives were like before they were lost, what their lives were like at sea, amidst that brotherhood that buoyed them even while they lived and worked with the uncertainty of ever seeing their homes and loved ones again.

In many respects, when I began this book, I was venturing into uncharted waters so far as my own historical undertakings are concerned, though I was aware from the age of eighteen that an ancestor of mine, Nicholas

Easton, had been lost at sea off the Cape of Good Hope. Perhaps it was his mere mention, a footnote really, on the gravestone of his remarried widow that reawakened my interest in how he and others lived during the age of sail. I hope then that I have conveyed a fair amount of what I learned on that journey.

CHAPTER 1

Early American Seafaring

B y 1700, the ship had become the engine of commerce, a machine of empire.[4] With the expansion of the Atlantic Trade, and the growing dependency of empires during this period upon the success of their commercial and naval fleets, the demand for ordinary and able-bodied seamen increased. This demand led ultimately to war of a kind among "rulers, planners, merchants, Captains, Naval officials, sailors, and other urban workers over the value and purposes of maritime labor."[5]

In the European empires, the press-gangs who would coerce or simply kidnap young men for labor on board a ship became a dreaded reality for the urban poor and ethnically diverse population of seaside communities. British attempts to press seamen into service in America often met with violence, though the practice continued until a few years before the revolution. Impression was, on both sides of the Atlantic, little more than slavery and meant almost certain death. Three out of five men pressed into service died within two years, with only one in five of the dead expiring in battle.[6]

While merchant ships recruited able-bodied seamen and inexperienced sailors, or "green hands," for low wages, the dynamic of the ship and conditions were similar. As these conditions ebbed and flowed, and the harsh reality of life aboard ship with its discipline and hard work took hold, desertion often thinned out a ship's crew. The belabored captains of merchant vessels would take on sailors in whatever port they could be found.

Men and boys set to sea for many reasons: abject poverty, an aversion to farm or factory labor or an escape from indentured work, or even from war.

A farm boy gazes wistfully out to sea in an illustration from Whittier's *Ballads of New England* (1870).

Crews were an amalgamation of races, cultures and beliefs. They lived in close quarters, working long hours together for months, if not a journey of three or four years, and often in situations where their very lives depended on each other's abject cooperation. This was the "wooden world" described by Richard Simson, a late seventeenth-century seafarer.

Atlantic seamen of this period would have included sailors of English, French, Dutch, Portuguese, Scandinavian, Scottish, Irish, Welsh, West Indian, African and Native American descent to fit out the crews of merchant ships, whaling vessels, privateers and slavers that sailed the routes around the world from Europe and North America.

In British North America, the availability of land and long-standing opportunity for independent living meant that the lure of the sea was long secondary to timber and farming ventures. Between 80 and 90 percent of the population worked in agriculture throughout the eighteenth century.[7] A decline in the economy in the 1740s displaced many youth, as well as older men, from the certainties they had expected, as land and labor were suddenly scarce—and so the sea beckoned. In the New England colonies, however, we find another story; one in which settlers were venturing onto the Atlantic and beyond, at an earlier period.

As historian Samuel Eliot Morison wrote, "God performed no miracle on the New England soil. He gave the sea."[8] In 1641, when civil war in England cut the flow of immigrants to the colonies, the price of home-grown products plummeted. In addition, Massachusetts governor John Winthrop wrote that "all foreign commodities grew scarce…These straits set our people on work to provide fish, clapboards, plank, etc…and to set out to the West Indies for trade."

Communities in the colony, beginning with Dorchester, sent fleets out to ply the trade of fishing. Gloucester, Scituate and Marblehead soon followed, the latter rocky peninsula becoming noted as a major exporter of "dun fish," a commodity created by alternately burying and drying large cod until the fish "mellowed sufficiently for the taste of Catholic Europe."[9]

Those first fishermen who settled outside of Boston were "trouble-some people" to the staid Puritans, remnants of the Church of England followers, who were often a "wicked and drunken crue."[10] At the height of the season along the coast, as far north as Maine and the Canadian Maritimes, fishermen "squatted in places that were of no use to the farmers, their property rights tenuous…they were more interested in sea than in land tenures, roaming the coasts and islands, frequently moving house and setting up fishing berths in summer months, leaving in the fall to sell their catch to English and New England merchants."[11]

The colony grew then into a cluster of seaside communities and farming villages close to shore. As Morison noted, "For over a century after the *Mayflower*'s voyage, few Massachusetts farms were more than thirty miles distant from tidewater, and all felt the ebb and flow of sea-borne commerce."[12]

Such commerce soon attracted those "villains of all nations" to the New England coast. Pirates appeared in great proliferation, and from Boston, Great Britain took steps to protect those ships trading along the coastline.

The first recorded pirate in these waters was Dixey Bull, the owner of a small vessel that engaged in honest trade up and down the coast. In Penobscot Bay, he was attacked by an armed crew of Frenchmen, and on his return to Boston, recruited his own crew, determined on revenge. He made quite an impression over the coming years, attacking French and then

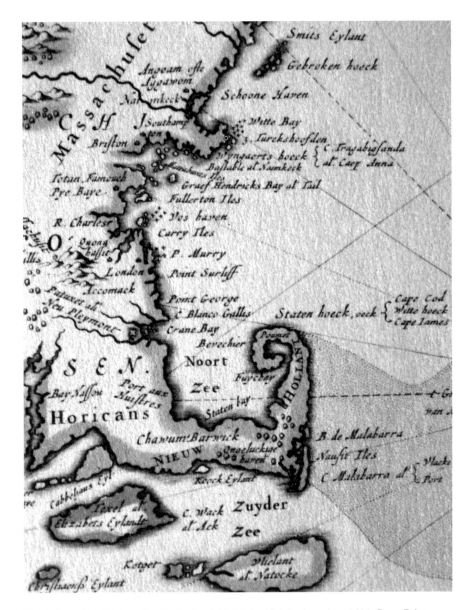

Detail from *New Belgium, New England and Virginia* by N. Visscher, circa 1682. Penn Prints, New York. *From the author's collection.*

English vessels plying the Atlantic. His boldest move came when he sailed a flotilla of three ships into Pemaquid Harbor in Maine and bombarded the fort there, eventually going ashore and plundering the town while its frightened residents hid in the woods. He is rumored to have buried much of the loot in Damaris Cove and on Cushing Island in Casco Bay.[13]

The guarding of the coast was appointed to Captain Cyprian Southack in 1692. He was employed "in the service of the Crown of Great Britain...to cruise about the Capes and convoy vessels from Virginia, Pennsylvania, Connecticut, etc., between Massachusetts, Martha's Vineyard, and Rhode Island."[14]

Southack also participated in a long series of expeditions to map the coastal waters of northern New England and Canada. He produced numerous manuscript maps, including *A Draught of Boston Harbor* and, more expansively, *A Draught of New England, Newfoundland, Nova Scotia, and the River of Canada by 1694*. His first published work, *A New Chart of the English Empire in America* (1717), established Southack's reputation as a cartographer, and continued expeditions led to the publication of his *New England Coasting Pilot* in 1729.

New Hampshire had been industrious in fishing since fleets set out from Portsmouth, where the Piscataqua River empties into the sea. Along the coast of what we now know as New Hampshire and Maine, from Bath and Brunswick to Kittery and Portsmouth, shipbuilding became a major industry. Even upriver villages like Dover and South Berwick harvested acres of white oak and white pine for shipbuilding, the tall pines especially being favored with shipbuilders for masts. In 1690, the first warship built in America, a 637-ton frigate named the *Faulkland*, was built on a wharf attached to a small island between Kittery and Portsmouth.[15]

This territory remained largely wilderness, the remains of failed settlements visible by those who used the waters for seasonal fishing or trade. The fishermen came as they had for generations to fill up their holds with cod and tataug before heading back to home ports. The traders tended to stay weeks during the summer, often laying anchor and conducting business on the nearest spit of land. As historian John Gillis writes, "The first seaports were not so much *of* the coasts as *on* the coasts. Many were located on actual islands, others on islandlike peninsulas. All were detached from the lands around them. Seaports like Boston had very shallow hinterlands, and some none at all."[16]

Despite all this activity, the coastline of Northern New England and Nova Scotia was barely known beyond the local mariners. Southack endeavored to change that and was not shy about proclaiming his exploits in letters. He understood that "public notices of his services were just as important as the services themselves."[17] In spite of this public bravado, his passages and descriptions in *New England Coasting Pilot* are often brief and taut as a mainsail's rope for what he must have witnessed.

Captain Southack, among other seasoned mariners, knew well the hardships of life on the sea. In the spring of 1717, he and his crew were sent to investigate the report of a pirate wreck off Eastham on Cape Cod. Southack and his crew reached the site through a long, narrow passage, now long filled in, that once crossed the Cape at its elbow, and arrived to find that the remains of the *Whidah* had been stripped of all that the sea hadn't taken. His report notes that the locals were less than helpful in news concerning the disaster, and he and his men "buried One Hundred and Two Men Drowned" who had washed ashore.

The captain and other literate mariners would also have known of the disaster of August 12, 1635, when the Reverend John Avery, with his wife and children, were "lost in a storm off Thatcher's Island," along with nineteen others, all but two from Ipswich and Marblehead. Southack likely read of the "miracle" of more recent times written in Cotton Mather's *Magnalia Christi Americana* (Works of Christ in America), which related an event in 1647 of the "apparition of a ship in the air."

It seems the January before, a ship had set sail with a "rich treasure of passengers" from New Haven on passage to England. When no word came of their arrival, the parishioners of the Reverend Mr. Davenport's flock sent "much prayer, both Publick and Private, that the Lord would...let them hear what he had done with their dear Friends, and prepare them with a suitable Submission to his Holy Will." One afternoon in June, after a particularly violent thunderstorm, and just as the sky was clearing about an hour before sunset, the apparition appeared:

> *Coming up from our Harbour's Mouth, which lyes southward from the Town, seemingly with her Sails filled under a fresh Gale, holding her Course North, and continuing under Observation, Sailing against the Wind for the space of half an Hour...At length, crouding up as far there is usually Water sufficient for such a Vessel, and so near some of the Spectators, as that they imagined a Man might hurl a stone on Board her, her Mainstop seem'd to be blown off, but left hanging in the Shrouds; then her Missen-top; then all her Masting seemed blown away by the Board...she overset and so vanished into a smoaky Cloud, which in some time dissipated, leaving, as everywhere else, a clear Air.*

These tales and many others that would likely have been read or related in the slew of taverns that hosted seamen in port cities did not for a whit deter men from signing aboard a ship. When one of the first ships built in

Frontispiece from Edward Barlow's journal. *From the author's collection.*

Illustration of early Newport, circa 1739. *Courtesy of the Rhode Island Historical Society.*

Boston, the *Trial*, recruited its crew, "the foremast hands were recruited in part from English seaports, but mostly from the adventure-loving youth of the colonies."[18] Rhode Island governor Samuel Cranston in 1708 wrote enthusiastically of the youth of the colony's "love of the sea."

By the early eighteenth century, a generation of Newporters would have known the nautical exploits of numerous pirates who had taken harbor along the coast, being among the "chiefe places where Pyrates Resort & are Harbored," as Edward Randolph had reported to British authorities. Men of their own native stock, most notably Thomas Tew, William Mayes, Joseph Banks and Thomas Wake, among others, had contributed to the growing lore.

Tew was captain aboard the *Amity*, a vessel that was hired in tandem with another sloop to attack a French factory on the German coast of Africa during King William's war in 1693. When the ships lost sight of each other after a violent storm, Tew gathered the crew together and proposed a change in plans, "a course which should lead them to ease and plenty."

The crew endorsed the captain's plan with enthusiasm and set the *Amity* to sail for the Cape of Good Hope and, from there, the beginnings of the Red Sea. In the Straits of Bab El Mandes, they came upon a "richly laden" vessel bound for Arabia. Despite being heavily guarded and gunned, the forty-five-man crew of the *Amity* quickly overtook the ship and seized its gold, silver and jewels, as well as gunpowder.[19]

Tew quickly made for the island of St. Mary's off Madagascar, where "twenty-three of the crew, following the quartermaster, decided to take their shares there, and to settle in this apparently idyllic spot."[20] When Tew and his remaining crew returned to Newport, he settled there "unquestioned," and his crew scattered. The spoils, it was rumored, were to have been as much as £12,000 for the captain and £3,000 for each man of the crew.

In the fall of 1694, the *Amity* was outfitting for another voyage, along with Mayes's sixty-ton brigantine built in Newport named the *Pearl*; Bankes's "plantation-built" bark, the *Portsmouth Adventure*; and Wake's bark, the *Susanna*, preparing for passage to the Red Sea. Tew's earlier success had a significant impact on the town. As Nathanial Coddington wrote, "Great was the Commotion whilst they lay here, Servants running from their Masters, sonns from their Parents and many had their Children and Relations going against their will."

The ships set sail with great celebration, and the convoy was joined off the coast of Delaware by the *Dolphin*, a Spanish-built brigantine commanded by Captain Want, a former member of Tew's crew aboard the *Amity*. It seems that despite Coddington's cautionary note that "many was the young men went out belonging to this place where some few returned," the lure of fortune had overtaken many in town.

Indeed, these ships were to have mixed results in their ventures, joining in tandem with pirate Captain Henry Every, a plunderer of some repute by the time the Newporters had met him in the Red Sea aboard the *Fancy*, a British man-of-war. Bankes assigned his commission to Joseph Faro, who then took command of the *Portsmouth Adventure*. They spent the summer at sea in fiercely hot conditions and heavy humidity, as well as squalls and sandstorms that plagued the crews.

In September, the convoy of pirates noticed an Indian fleet of twenty-five ships sailing from the Small Strait off Mocha and began pursuit. It was clear from the beginning of the campaign that the Newport ships were outclassed by the man-of-war and struggled to keep company. The *Dolphin* was in Every's eyes "an ill sayler" and so was burned by the pirate and the crew taken aboard the *Fancy*. The *Pearl* had to be towed, and Captain Tew's *Amity* "fell asterne and never came up to them," while Captain Wake in the *Susannah* struggled to keep the *Fancy*'s pace. Only the *Portsmouth Adventure* seems to have joined the chase without incident. In three days, the convoy had overtaken a vessel belonging to "the richest merchant of Surat" and took as much as £60,000 in silver and gold.[21]

The convoy made landfall near Bombay and soon spied another large vessel, which proved to be the *Gunj-I sawai* (*Esteemed Treasure*), a royal ship belonging to Aurangzeb, the "Great Mogul" or Emperor of Hindustan. After a brief battle, Every's crew boarded the ship to find concubines bound for the Mogul's harem dressed in turbans with swords in hand, placed in battle by the panic-stricken Indian captain. The pirates soon made short order of the ship's defenses and, once the ship was taken, spent days aboard, searching for treasure and taking their pleasure with those ladies who had not leapt overboard or taken their own lives to protect their loyalty to the Great Mogul.

It remains unclear how many ships in Every's convoy took place in the looting, though the official East India Company documents state that the *Gunj-I sawai* "was attacked by "four English ships." Only William Mayes and his crew aboard the *Pearl* received a share of the booty, though the *Amity* seems also to have been engaged as she limped into port at St. Mary's in mid-December, "having no Captain, her former Captain Tew being killed by a great shott from a Moor's Ship." Captain Wake, whose ship the *Susannah* had arrived just days before the *Amity*, languished in port until spring while the captain and much of the crew died from disease. The remaining crew sailed the ship to St. Augustine and joined another convoy on the Red Sea. Mayes reportedly sailed the *Pearl* for Ethiopia and remained out of sight for years—until July 1699, when a report came that a ship had been spotted off the coast of Massachusetts whose captain was said to be "one Maise, a Pyrate who has brought a vast deale of wealth from the red Seas."[22] He eventually returned to Newport, where in 1702, he procured a license to "sell strong drinke" in the house he had inherited from his father.[23] Faro sailed the *Portsmouth Adventure* to the Persian Gulf, taking some compensation for keeping Every's ship company, though reputedly having "never come into the Fight."

Maritime historian Alexander Boyd Hawes wrote, "Piracy continued as an important industry through the 1690s. Pirates fitted out and obtained commissions there. Rhode Islanders signed up as pirate crew members. Various pirates chose Rhode Island as a refuge. And a few, though this was rare and of little significance, were arrested in the Colony."[24]

Perhaps the most famous pirate associated with Rhode Island waters is William Kidd, who had been commissioned in January 1696 by Peter Cooke, the Earl of Bellomont, and other London investors to find and capture Captains Tew, Mayes, Every and others. He was also given license to attack French vessels at will. The London financers paid for most of the expedition, but Kidd had to raise money himself to obtain the ship and the handpicked crew he wanted.

When all was in order, he set forth in the *Adventure Galley*, weighing over 284 tons burthen, with thirty-four cannon aboard and equipped with oars for maneuvering in battle.

But Captain Kidd's first venture on behalf of the British investors began badly when, after he neglected to salute a navy yacht in Greenwich as he headed down the Thames, he was fired upon and then his ship boarded, with much of his crew arrested and pressed into naval service. The young captain was indignant and soon resolved to join the ranks of those he had agreed to capture. Kidd left short-handed for New York but captured a French vessel along the way to obtain enough goods to hire another crew. It was with that crew—said later in court to be mostly hardened and well-feared criminals—that his career as a pirate began, and the captain soon gained a reputation as a sharp-minded and fearless leader in attacks on Mughal and French convoys.

The pirate life was still a mariner's life, and Kidd reputedly lost a third of his crew to cholera on the way to the Cape of Good Hope. He sailed fruitlessly for months in search of new crewmen, even as some deserted ship and others threatened mutiny if the tide did not turn soon. Then in January 1698, Kidd and his crew captured an Armenian ship, the *Quedagh Merchant*, off Catalina Island, which proved to be filled with gold and silver, as well as luxuriant satins, muslins and valuable silks. The English captain of the vessel had documents giving the vessel French protection, but Kidd kept these and the loot, releasing the captain, and word soon made it back to England confirming that Kidd had turned pirate.

The stories connecting William Kidd and his treasure with Rhode Island come from his visit there in the summer of 1699. Making his way back from the West Indies, he steered his schooner through the west passage of Narragansett Bay to avoid Newport harbor and rounded the northern end of Conanicut Island, where his old friend Thomas Paine, and a former captain of the *Pearl*, kept a farm he called "Cajacet."

Kidd sent a boat ashore to summon Paine, and he was rowed back to the pirate's ship, where Kidd welcomed him and requested that he keep "some things" for him. Paine protested, as he later recalled in a deposition, "that his house would be searched," and indeed it was some weeks later by Cooke himself. While the search yielded nothing but a small amount of gold that Paine claimed was a "gift" from the pirate, the Earl was unconvinced. Of his visit and investigation into the colony's "irregularities," Cooke wrote, "When I was at Rhode Island, there was one Palmer a Pyrat who was out on bail, for they cannot be persuaded to keep a pyrat in Gaol: they love 'em too much."

It was later learned that Paine had, in fact, sent secreted amounts of gold to Sarah Kidd in Boston several times when requested. Local lore has the captain stopping at Block Island as well, presumably on his exodus after visiting Paine, where he was supplied by the family of James Sands, another well-known mariner. When it came time to pay, legend has it that the captain bid Sands's daughter Mercy Raymond to hold out her apron and filled it with gold and jewels.

Captain Kidd was also familiar with Hannah Screecham, a woman who lived alone on an island off the town of Cotuit, Massachusetts. Local lore tells us that the island was originally inhabited by Hannah and her sister Sarah but that after a rift between the siblings, Sarah had gone to Mashpee to continue her practice of witchcraft. She lived alone in the woods by a body of water that came to be known as Witches Pond. Hannah stayed on the island and befriended the numerous pirates who passed by. Over the years, Kidd, Black Bellamy, Paul Williams and other pirates came to trust Hannah Screecham and to entrust their gold to her keeping.

According to Mashpee Wampanoag legend, a pirate sloop would anchor within sight of the island and fly a signal flag while a boat was put out with the captain and his treasure, and one sailor to row them to shore. Each time this occurred, with Kidd and others,

> *Hannah went down to the sea-beach, kissed the Captain, and nodded to the sailor. The Captain gave her a shawl, or a locket of hair, or a finger ring. At her direction, the sailor carried the treasure into the interior of the island where a deep pit had been dug. When the last bar was laid in place, and the last coin safe in its box, Hannah pushed the sailor into the yawning pit. Quick-running sands seeped over him, and he was buried alive. Then she screamed like the gull in the storm, a cry that mingled with the wind in the stunted trees, or the waves shrilling on the outer beach. At that signal, the Captain put back to his ship; and even the…cruelest of buccaneers, shivered as he heard her wail. Yet he knew that his treasure was safe, its whereabouts known to only two, Hannah Screecham and himself.*[25]

William Kidd was eventually arrested in Boston with his wife. Also taken were part of his crew, who were then shipped, along with accused pirates Joseph Palmer, Joseph Bradish and James Gillam, to face trials in London. It was Palmer's testimony in court concerning Kidd's fatal strike with an iron-bound bucket on the head of gunner Michael Moore some years before that led to a conviction of murder and his execution in 1701.

Though these captures and executions were highly touted by British authorities, it did little to stem the wave of sailors drawn by the hope of fortune. The industry of privateering was to thrive for many years out of Newport Harbor and the surrounding seaside communities. An advertisement in the *Boston News-Letter* from 1704 proclaimed, "Capt. Peter Lawrence is going a Privateering from Rhode Island, in a good sloop, about 60 tons, six guns, and 90 men for Canada and any gentlemen or sailors that are disposed to go will be kindly entertained."

Forty years later, when Scottish physician and philosopher Alexander Hamilton eagerly attended a meeting of the "Philosophical Club" in Newport, the follower of European enlightenment recorded that he "was surprised to find that no matters of philosophy were brought upon the carpet. They talked of privateering and building vessels."[26]

Privateer crews were made up of both ordinary seamen and "landsmen"—those marksmen and gunners who chose to take the added risk those various skirmishes encountered on the voyage would bring in

The USS *Revenge*, a Rhode Island privateer. *Courtesy of the Rhode Island Historical Society.*

exchange for higher wages and a share of the "Prize." Howard M. Chapin would write in his *Rhode Island Privateers* that these vessels often held a crew of one hundred or more.

In spite of the size of the crew, a privateering ship was an island of capitalism, and some historians argue that it was aboard such vessels that the first tenets of social democracy were drawn within the contracts that bound the owner of a privateering ship and its commander to the concern of every member of the crew.

When the Newport privateer *Revenge* sailed under Captain James Allen in September 1743, its "Articles of Agreement" included among its twenty-one provisions not only the basic rules to maintain order aboard a vessel but also the appointment of a "Committee" headed up by the captain and members of the crew to "manage all matters and affairs relating to the voyage." There were also provisions that dealt specifically with injury and death to the ordinary seaman: "13. If any one of the Company happens to loose a joint or joints in the time of Engagement, he shall receive, and have out of the Prize, One hundred pieces of Eight for each joint so lost; or if he happens to loose his limb, he shall receive and have out of the Prize, six hundred pieces of Eight, or Six good and able Negroes, if the Prize taken amount to so much."[27]

The articles also provided for the sailor or landsman's family should death occur, stating that "the Prize or prizes taken before or at the time of his Death, his share, or shares thereof, shall be paid to his Executor or Administrator."

If the British authorities succeeded in ridding the Atlantic of a few famed pirates, historian James C. Johnston Jr. notes that "there were a lot of other freebooters willing to take prizes up and down the Atlantic Coast. Ships from Philadelphia, the largest and richest colonial center, and the rich trading vessels passing in and out of the harbor of New York were also sure to receive the attention of pirates." In Bristol, Rhode Island, Simeon Potter, "after a comparatively few years spent on the ocean," made a quick fortune as a privateer and returned to town "with a purse overflowing with riches, a man to be looked up to for the rest of his life."[28]

The stories and adventures related in the taprooms and taverns of the port towns surely contributed to the almost constant flow of New England men over the coming generations who were willing to go to sea. Written testimonies, too, soon had their influence. As more mariners became literate in the eighteenth century, the proliferation of published pamphlets and early travel narratives, especially from Great Britain, increased accordingly. From William Dampier's *A New Voyage Around the World* (1697) to accounts by Edward Cooke and Woodes Rogers in 1712, these works soon acquired an extensive following on both sides of the Atlantic. Amid these memoirs and tales of travel emerged a new genre of fiction based on seafaring adventures and those "remarkable occurrences" chronicled in the newspapers of the period. An early author of these tales was Daniel Defoe, a sometime journalist and novelist from Great Britain who received wide readership in America.

Though not credited on the title page, Defoe is widely believed to be the author of the immensely popular *A General History of the Pyrates* (1724), though

Silver bowl belonging to Simeon Potter from his privateering days. *Courtesy of the Rhode Island Historical Society.*

certainly the most popular among his attributed books was *The Life and Strange Surprising Adventures of Robinson Crusoe of York, Mariner* (1719). Defoe's tale is of an admitted "adventurer" who goes to sea to seek his fortune but whose inexperience leads to misfortune, until he begins to learn the mariner's craft under the tutelage of an old salt with a soft heart. After the captain who befriended him dies, Crusoe sets out on his own in the African trade. He is soon captured and imprisoned and then sold into slavery.

Despite these setbacks, Crusoe never wavers in his diligence, and after two long years in captivity, thinking of "nothing but my Escape; and what Method I might take to effect it," he seizes his opportunity when his master

The gravestone of Sylvanus Hopkins, North Burial Ground, Providence, Rhode Island. *Photo courtesy of the author.*

outfits a boat, and he soon hijacks the craft to seek freedom along the African coast.[29] A shipwreck that follows at literally the edge of the map lets Crusoe practice the skills through which he has matured yet again, creating a domain of his own on an isolated isle in which he thrives until rescue and the return home to unexpected fortune.

The reality was often very different, as anyone knowing the story of the brig *Polly* will remember. The ship sailed from Boston in December 1811, bound for Santa Cruz with salted provisions and lumber. It carried a small crew, Captain W.L. Cazneau, a mate, four crewmen and a native American cook. There were also two passengers aboard, a nine-year-old African American girl and her charge, Mr. J.S. Hunt. Captain Cazneau successfully cleared the dreaded Cape Cod and the hidden reefs of the Georges, after which they could set their course southward into the milder waters of the Gulf Stream.

Less than a week out, however, a sudden storm from the southeast overwhelmed the *Polly*, shredding its sails and finally throwing the ship on its beam-ends about midnight. The crew clung to the rigging and tried to cut away the tangled spars and ropes and hacked away at the mainmast and foremast in an effort to right the brig. They succeeded, and all the crew survived, but Mr. Hunt had been swept overboard, and the girl, who had clung to the skylight inside the cabin when the water rolled in, died just a few hours after rescue.

The men recovered some of the salted provisions from the hold and a keg of fresh water was found lashed to the quarterdeck, but the rest of the water casks had been smashed or washed away. They were now adrift, helpless in the currents of the Atlantic. The cask of water lasted for eighteen days. An occasional rain would replenish the barrel, but after forty days, all the salted provisions were gone. Worse still, the *Polly* was drifting farther from the trade routes and the chance of a rescue.

On the fiftieth day adrift, the crew suffered the first death aboard the ship when the mate Mr. Paddock died. Six days later, a young seaman named Howe expired. With an uncanny will to survive, the captain devised an apparatus for distilling seawater on the oven in the galley, and thereafter, the men methodically brought up buckets of seawater to obtain a few glasses of drinking water a day. Nonetheless, on March 15, after three months adrift, the Native American cook "gave up the ghost, evidently from want of water, though with much less distress than the others, and in the full exercise of his reason."

In April, another seaman named Johnson died. The brig continued to drift into the area known as the Sargasso Sea, long known to be a near-windless expanse of stagnant ocean between the Azores and Antilles, where currents circle confusingly and sailing ships can languish for weeks. However, to the remaining men of the floating hulk that had once been the *Polly*, the warm waters were a boon of fishing and catching crab. Renewed, they built a shelter with the timber from the hold and even set out fish to dry in the tropical sun. By June, however, another seaman had died, and there was only the captain and Samuel Badger left aboard.

The men drifted back into the trade waters of the Atlantic, maintaining a routine of distilling seawater and catching fish when possible. The men occasionally spied sails on the horizon, but none came near the drifting derelict. The battered ship drifted toward the Canary Islands and would have drifted eventually onto the coast of Africa, when it was finally spied by three ships, and a boat was dropped from ship *Fame* from Hull, Massachusetts, to rescue the captain and surviving crewmember. The *Polly* had drifted for 192 days[30] and an old narrative records, "Every attention was paid to the sufferers that generosity warmed with pity and fellow-feeling could dictate, on board the Fame. They were transferred from this ship to the brig *Dromio* and arrived in the United States in safety."

Countless tales of ill-gotten voyages abounded in the taverns and harbor masters' quarters of that time. Though now most are forgotten, a hint of these stories can be found in the graveyards of seaside communities, as with the memorial stone of young Silvanus Hopkins in Providence's North Burial Ground. The stone tablet affixed to the monument tells the viewer that the son of Rhode Island's illustrious governor, and signer of the Declaration of Independence

was cast away
on Cape Breton shore &
inhumanely murdered
by cruel savages on
the 23rd of April 1753.
Aged 18 years 5 months
And 23 days

CHAPTER 2

Preparing to Sail

In preparing for a journey, the educated captains and mates of a ship would be sure that whatever maps, charts and pilot books needed for the voyage were up to date, as well as make sure they had the latest in technology that was available. A well-worn copy of James Atkinson's *Epitome of the Art of Navigation* or Nathanial Colson's *A Mariner's Guide* would be common reading in a captain's library, and works like Haselden's popular *Seamens Daily Assistant* could be found in any able-bodied seaman's chest. Technology, too, had its evolving instruments for soundings, measuring distance and orientation, as well as for gauging the weather.

By 1750, for instance, "storm-bottles" would have been in use aboard most vessels. These hermetically sealed glass tubes contained water, alcohol and camphor, and their crystals fell to the bottom of the tubes in improving weather but rose when an impending tempest was at hand. In 1759, John Harrison perfected the use of the marine chronometer, allowing captains for the first time to calculate longitude at sea. By the later part of the eighteenth century, a captain would have to be proficient in using not only the compass and telescope but also the sextant, quadrant and chronometer, as well as having studied the navigational maps, if not already having a firsthand knowledge of the surrounding waters, entrances and harbors on the ship's manifest. While captains often hired local pilots to bring ships safely in and out of harbors, they studied navigation as well, for there could well be a time when they would have to make port on their own.

Sailing ships followed the trade winds that had been used for centuries, and experienced shipmasters could use the regular and seasonal winds to make long and profitable passages in a short amount of time.[31]

As many merchant captains were sons of established mariners, these young men were already well schooled by the time they acquired command of their own ships. Often, several members of a family, as with the Brown brothers of Providence, were at sea on separate ships and voyages for successive years.

Cartography, science and experience aside, captains were not above seeking spiritual help or having a horoscope prepared before an impending voyage, as Captain David Lindsay of Newport had done before sailing the brigantine *Sanderson* in 1752.

Life on board the ship for ordinary and able-bodied seamen began the moment they signed on. A Rhode Island brig for the Havana trade would have carried six hands, and a brig used in the slave trade would have employed nine or ten hands (if some of those hands were not slaves themselves), including a first and second mate, five seamen, a cooper and a cook.[32]

In the traditional hierarchy that came to be the way of a ship, individual sailors were considered "ordinary" seamen, that is, lacking at least some of those skills acquired by the more experienced or "able-bodied" seamen. Young sailors, or "green hands" would first be taught fundamental ship handling: the navigation of the vessel; the making and taking in of sail; steering the ship; trimming sails; learning the lines and their purposes in the rigging; and getting firsthand knowledge of tackling, purchasing and anchoring techniques.

Learning to maintain the ship was of equal importance. As historian W. Jeffrey Bolster writes, "Sailors worked relentlessly to halt nature's assault on their vessels. They scraped and sanded then oiled and painted their ship's wooden planks. They slushed masts and tarred shrouds. They payed pitch into deck seams and filled checks in yards or gaffes. They replaced old rigging with new, which they fabricated on board, reeving lanyards, and constantly heaving taut rigging made slack by the ocean's ceaseless swell."[33]

Aboard the vessel, chores needing multiple hands were meted out with sea shanties devised for specific tasks. Sea shanties were sung aboard every sailing vessel, with the exception of the navy ships. Silence aboard a man-of-war was essential in order to hear commands, and meant the difference between life and death when moving into battle. Tight discipline, constant drum and spoken cadence commands took the place of shanties.[34]

Sailors aboard merchant, whaling and slaving vessels sung out four distinct types of shanties. Each had its own beat and tempo for its task, with

Mystic Fishing Schooner, undated, painted by Captain Ellery F. Thompson.

the sailors' singing chorus to the shantyman's line sung out—a method that helped the hands perform the work efficiently.

The capstan or windlass shanties were employed in weighing anchor, as well as in loading and unloading the ship. As folklorist Duncan Emrich explains, "The shantyman sat on the capstan head or stood to one side of the deck while the sailors pushed on the capstan bars, turning the capstan slowly to the rhythmic beat of the song."[35] Capstan shanties were considered to be the most tuneful and were often built on a story line due to the length of the task. An example would be the shanty "Rolling Home," a long-used shanty on the Atlantic whose lyrics were adapted for New England sailors:

> *Pipe all hands to man the windlass,*
> *See our cable run down clear,*
> *As we heave away our anchor,*
> *For New England's shores we'll steer.*
> *Rolling home, rolling home,*
> *Rolling home across the sea,*
> *Rolling home to New England,*
> *Rolling home, dear land to thee.*[36]

The frontispiece from Chapelle's *The History of American Sailing Ships.*

Halyard or long-haul shanties were used with heavy work that demanded a long pull, such as the hoisting of a yard or sail. These were also lengthy due to the time-consuming task but emphasized two heavily accented beats in the chorus lines of each stanza when the men hoisted the rope in unison, allowing sailors to rest between beats and then pull again:

A Yankee ship came down the river,
Blow, boys, blow,
And how do you know she's a Yankee Clipper?
Blow, boys, blow,
Oh, how do you know she's a Yankee Clipper?
Blow, boys, blow.[37]

By contrast to the first two shanties, the short-haul shanty was a brief song used for the short, hard tasks such as bunting up a sail after it was furled or hauling aft the foresheet. It gave only one accented beat, with the pull performed on the last word of each stanza:

Hail the bowline, the long-tailed bowline,
Hail the bowline, the bowline, haul!
Hail the bowline, we'll haul for better weather,
Hail the bowline, the bowline, haul![38]

The last type of shanty used was called a walkaway, used as a hand-over-hand shanty when hoisting a light sail or as a song employed in cleaning the weeds and barnacles from the ship—a task where the rope was thrown over the stern and marched on each side in unison to the bow, with the rope scraping the bottom of the boat during the march to the song's cadence. The most common of this type of shanty was "The Drunken Sailor," known even to landlubbers:

Now what shall we do with the drunken sailor,
What shall we do with the drunken sailor,
What shall we do with the drunken sailor
Early in the morning?

Oh, chuck him in the long boat till he gets sober,
Chuck him in the long boat till he gets sober,
Chuck him in the longboat till he gets sober
Early in the morning.

Ay hey and up she rises,
Ay hey and up she rises,
Ay hey and up she rises
Early in the morning.[39]

For whaling vessels, there were other chores for the crew. Harpoons, lances and spades all had to be sharpened to a fine-honed edge and then carefully stored for their next use. Lines were coiled in tubs, and oars and paddles were repaired and oiled for the whaleboats. In good weather, the green hands were lowered in boats and instructed by the older seamen on the maneuvering and skills needed to procure a whale in open water.

A Westerly Whaler, built for the New Bedford fleet. *From* Sailing Ships of New England.

In rough weather, it was up to those with "sailorizing" skills to teach the younger hands the intricate knots used in securing the sails and cargo during a storm. What couldn't be controlled by skills or any human effort were those "remarkable occurrences," for which only precautions of faith could be taken.

Aboard each vessel, there were well-known and time-borne traditions: no ship ever sailed on a Friday, and the ringing of bells, aside from the ship's bell, was forbidden, as were flowers aboard a ship, for their association with funerals.

Several historians I have read in preparing this work have stated that priests and clergy were equally unwelcome for the same association, but there seems ample evidence that by the period of the "great awakening"

A drawing of the elaborate figurehead of the *Queen Charlotte* (1790) from L.G. Carr Laughton's *Old Ship Figureheads & Sterns.*

in the 1740s, ministers like the Quaker John Woolman and the English evangelist George Whitfield were preaching aboard vessels during their travels and passing out Bibles to the crew. Just the same, a captain might affix a coin to the mast, and seamen would circle the base with coins as an offering for a safe journey or at least a journey across the river Styx.

A ship might even be adorned at the bow with the figurehead of a well-endowed maiden, often bare-breasted, especially if it were a British vessel. More staid American ship owners adorned the masthead with equally endowed but fully clothed maidens who gazed earnestly ahead from the bowsprit. These carved figurines faced outward with purpose, in consort with the sailors' belief that a woman's breasts calmed the waves and thus kept the crew safe from harm. If an infant were born and thereby nursed aboard the ship, it was sure to bring good fortune.

Of course, there were many types of figureheads during the age of sail. Early figureheads included dragons and horse's heads. Royalty often outfitted their fleet with elaborate figureheads made up of horses, lions, princely figures and cherubic trumpeters. By the nineteenth century, many merchant vessels, especially, were adorned with figureheads connected to some vanity of the ship's owner. Remarkably, however, the maiden motif born of this superstition remained in some form aboard most wooden vessels, whether carved in relief along the stern or rails or on the hanging pieces of naval ships.

It was an old superstition that it was bad luck to rename a ship, and perhaps the same might be said for changing figureheads. When Providence merchant Suchaut Mauran II had a ship of 991 tons built in 1758 at a boatyard in Quincy, Massachusetts, he chose to adorn the vessel with a carving of a mournful-looking maiden originally salvaged from the French warship *Berceau*, captured by the American frigate *Boston* after a skirmish during the brief alliance with Britain against the French, earlier in the century. The figurehead had since adorned a ship called the *Caroline*, which had been wrecked in a storm, but the maiden was salvaged again and found a home on the bowsprit of Mauran's ship the *Maritana*.

The ship plied the Atlantic for several uneventful years until the afternoon of November 2, 1861, when it returned to New England waters, headed for Boston with a full cargo of steel, iron, coal, potash and wool. Captain Williams spotted Highland Light on Cape Cod around 4:30 p.m. Four hours later, the *Maritana* took a bearing on Race Point Light and continued its course for Boston Harbor. While still far out on the bay, the ship sailed into a southeasterly gale. Keeping course, the determined captain finally caught a brief glimpse of Boston Light around midnight, before the snow fell thick and furious,

The figurehead of the *Maritana*, from Edward R. Snow's *Storms and Shipwrecks of New England*.

obscuring any view. The crew was ordered to tack, but before the ship could be brought into the wind, it became caught in the breakers and dragged onto Shag Rocks, half a mile east of the light.

Once on the rocks, a heavy sea pounded the ship repeatedly, and the captain sensed quickly that the ship was doomed. He made efforts to remove the passengers and crew, but a longboat sent over the side was immediately stove in, and other boats were "crushed to pieces in the davits."[40] A seaman named Thomas Haney swam ashore with a line but could not climb high enough on the rocks to escape the tide and so was dragged back to the stricken ship.

By 3:00 a.m., the masts had been cut off and the vessel ground against the rocks as the tide receded. When the strain became too great, the vessel broke in two, sending Captain Williams tumbling to his death. In the ensuing hours, the remaining passengers and crew fought for their lives. Seven passengers clung to part of the poop deck, which had come free and made it to shore. Five of the crew also swam to Shag Rocks and managed to climb up out of reach of the sea.

When the storm began to lift, the ship could finally be seen from Boston Light, though Keeper Moses Barrett knew that a lifeboat could not be sent out until the waves subsided. He raised up a distress signal flag that he hoped would be noticed across the lighthouse channel in Hull, even though the flag was shredded by the winds within minutes. By 2:00 p.m. on the afternoon of the November 3, a dory was sent out from the lifesaving station at Hull, and the survivors on Shag Rocks were finally rescued. In all, twenty-six others had drowned, making it the worst disaster to occur in Boston Harbor. For days afterward, the islands of the harbor were littered with bodies and debris.

The figurehead was salvaged yet again and brought to Lincoln Pier in Boston, which caught fire soon after. Those with a superstitious inclination blamed the figurehead for the shipwreck and the fire, and the anxious-looking maiden was retired and is now preserved in the Marine Room of the Old State House.

The sailors who made up the crews of the traders, privateers, whalers and slave ships that plied the Atlantic in the age of sail held a myriad of rituals and superstitions, related to the hard-worn beliefs clung to by their brotherhood. They expressed these beliefs in a number of ways.

Before going aboard ship, the sailor might "cast off" his overalls and coats worn in the fields. He might even throw his shoes overboard as a sign of bondage to the sea. Tattoos were a lucky talisman from the early days of sail. By the eighteenth century, many a mariner would have been witness to those sailors from the South Sea Island's method of pricking their skin with a flame-blackened sharp stick and then rubbing in gunpowder to finish the work, which was often of simple design.

The "Jerusalem Cross" was a common adornment, and Catholics especially marked themselves with a cross near the heart or on the shoulder. Protestants did not display the cross as a symbol on the body, but a fish, the symbol taken by early Christians, was also a common mark. Seamen of both faiths, no doubt, had in mind incidents like the one written of by Barlow: "Our carpenter, who was cast away with me on the Goodwin Sands, fell very sick and died; and when he was dead, they would not let us bury him in, or near the city, for the reason that protestants are not worthy of burial, or at least not worthy to lie near where the papist is buried; so we carried him five or six miles by water and buried him near the seaside where few come."[41]

Able-bodied seamen or rovers, as they often called themselves—those sailors who signed aboard ship after ship and traveled the world—often adorned their heads, necks and shoulders with tattoos. Sometimes the entire figure of a woman would be replicated on the arm.[42] Naval men traditionally had ships and anchors tattooed on their bodies. Coopers might have a barrel tattoo. Other trades adapted symbols as well, as a form of identification, and African sailors and natives from the South Seas these sailors encountered had body markings as well to indicate the places from which they came, as well as family ancestry.

The most common symbol associated with marine lore, especially pirates, is the "death's head": a white skull and crossbones that adorned a black ensign and was commonly flown by many vessels. This symbol was taken from the tradition of drawing a skull in the margins of the daily entry in the ship's log to indicate a death at sea.

Around the ship, there were precautions, too, that must be taken: a hatch or basin placed upside down represented a sinking ship, and dropping the hatch into the hold foretold of greater disaster. An empty coffin aboard meant that it would soon be filled by an unlucky member of the crew. Killing of a dolphin, gull or albatross by any member of the crew was thought to be a harbinger of ill luck, the latter most notably expressed in Coleridge's "The Rhyme of the Ancient Mariner."

Perhaps the most commonly related ritual or set of rituals to pass from a sailor's life to the reading public has been those associated with a ship "crossing the line" of the equator. Ceremonies aboard merchant and privateer vessels took on elaborate pageantry and dance, as well as practical jokes on the green hands aboard. The journal of the Rhode Island privateer *Yankee* gives us a glimpse into these ceremonies:

> 20th Day Friday 6th Nov. At 1 p.m. being in Lat. 22. 49', the Crew of the *Yankee* preparing to celebrate Old Neptune's ceremonies on passing the Tropics. Accordingly, the old Sea God attended by his Lady, barbers and constables, dressed in the most fantastic manner, with painted faces, and swabs upon their heads, hailed our brig, came on board, were received with a salute and three cheers... The several candidates for a seaman's character were properly painted, slushed, shaved, ducked, questioned and sworn... After the ceremony concluded, the Commander, Officers, and whole crew joined in a Ducking match.[43]

It appears that on some vessels, those sailors crossing the equator for the first time were given a choice to pay a fine or submit themselves to a dunking in the deep. The journal of Francis Rogers describes the fate of those who refused to pay:

> Five of our men, not being willing to pay a bottle of brandy and a pound of sugar, were ducked according to custom... The manner of ducking is this; there is a block made fast to the main yard arm, through which is reeved a long rope, one end whereof comes down on the Quarter Deck, the other to the water, at which end is made fast a stick about a foot and a half long thwartways, on which the person sits across, holding fast with his hands the rope as it goes up having a running knot about him; when being ready he is hoisted up close to the yard arm, by the people on the Quarter Deck, and at once let run. His own weight from that height plunges him under the water as low as the ship's keel; then they run him up again as fast as they can and so serve him three times, then he is free and may drink with the others that paid.[44]

Detail from a painting by J. Spin showing the ship *Leodes* of Boston during a storm on February 17, 1856. Reprinted in *Sailing Ships of New England*, Marine Research Society, 1924.

Despite this being an "old seaman's custom" for generations of mariners, by 1839, when Francis Allen Olmstead was writing aboard the whaling vessel *North American*, he noted that despite his own intrigue with those "disagreeable ceremonies" that initiated green hands into "the mysteries of Neptune," "these…ceremonies which were formally observed very generally, have for the most part become disused. On board the *North American*, nothing of the kind was tolerated."[45]

Sailors also adopted weather-related superstitions. Clapping hands aboard a ship was thought to bring thunder, and throwing stones into the sea could bring on huge swells.[46] Animals could also indicate changes in weather. Porpoises, for instance, swimming in herds on both sides of the ship was long seen as "the forerunner of a gale of wind,"[47] and the prevailing storm would come from the direction in which they swam, as it was well known that the "seahogs" always headed into the current of an oncoming storm.

"Red sky in the morning, sailors take warning. Red sky at night, sailors delight" is perhaps the most commonly known of nautical euphemisms, and it came from the sailors along the English coast, whose weather patterns come from the west, thereby when the air is clear, sunset will be tinted red.

In the morning, a reddish light would be reflected from clouds in the west, indicating that a storm would be approaching.

The moon was also a signal of the coming weather, with a greenish tint presaging "some days of fair weather."[48] A ring around the moon, however, was a gale warning. Most seamen also believed that if any bad weather were to come, it would be in the days preceding or following the change of the moon. The heavens also held portents of weather—a star following a rising moon meant certain bad weather, while comets could mean either good or bad fortune.

Seasoned sailors were also quick to spy a "wind dog"—an incomplete rainbow, which also meant an approaching storm.[49] The glowing, fire-like mass called "St. Elmo's fire" was another natural phenomenon thought by sailors to be an omen. Often appearing after a storm, these corposants were interpreted over the centuries by mariners as everything from the embodiment of Castor and Pollux during ancient times to the Holy Spirit or even the earthbound spirits of drowned comrades in the age of sail. As a ship entered the mass, what conspired could also bring omens. A light settling about the main topmast was interpreted as good fortune, whereas if a corposant settled like "a great glow-worm"[50] on deck, it was a bad sign.

This phenomena had been recorded in Atlantic waters since 1609, when William Stratchey, secretary-elect of Virginia, recorded in his journal aboard the *Sea Venture* during a rough stretch of weather when the sky was so black that "not a starre by night, no sunbeame by day was to be seen." Yet on the third night, the mate on watch "had an apparition of a little round light, like a faint starre, trembling, and streaming along with a sparkling blaze, half the height upon the mainmast, and shooting something from shroud to shroud."[51]

Other natural phenomena affected sailors as well. "Sea smoke," or vapors caused by a cold wind passing over warm waters, was also a dreaded occurrence and as dangerous in the shipping lanes on open water as the coastal fogs that hid treacherous rocks from the sailor's sight. As many New England whalers were sent to Antarctica, the surreal seascape itself was disorientating, and the same conditions could shroud icebergs from view.

Whatever precautions were taken, gales, storms and even hurricanes were certainties on any Atlantic voyage, especially through the long winters. For mariners, there was always the unforeseen, and in spite of the captains' and mates' faith in science and their instruments, every able-bodied seaman on deck kept a sharp eye on the horizon.

CHAPTER 3

Perils at Sea

Whatever reasons compelled men to go to sea, "a ship at sea was a dangerous place to work and live, even when activities were limited to the mundane. Traumatic injury was common. Drowning was always a possibility, for most seamen were poor swimmers at best."[52]

In fact, so fatalistic was the majority of seamen's views that if a sailor was taken overboard in rough weather, a line might not even be thrown. Some saw such a death as preordained, and the more superstitious among sailors might believe that one crew member sacrificed would save the rest in a later storm. "What the Sea wants, the Sea will have" was a common expression.

By the end of the eighteenth century, shipwrecks off the Massachusetts coast remained the primary cause of death among the state's merchant mariners. "Peaked Hill Bar," extending from Barnstable toward the tip of Cape Cod, took a great number of ships, even after the installation of Highland Light on the bluffs of Truro, "for no light could penetrate the fog, rain, and snowstorms that inflict our coast," as historian and navigator Samuel Eliot Morison wrote. Merchant vessels traveling during the winter months were especially vulnerable. Ralph D. Paine wrote in *Lost Ships and Lonely Seas*, "Mariners were profoundly grateful when they had safely worked offshore in the winter-time and were past Cape Cod, which bore a very evil repute in those days of square-rigged vessels."

One particular tragedy involving the Cape occurred in the winter of 1802, when three ships—the *Brutus, Ulysses* and *Volusia*—left Salem in tandem for European ports and were wrecked together the next day off the coast.

A sailboat tossed in rough weather. *Illustration from Whittier's* Ballads of New England.

"The fate of those who were washed ashore alive was most melancholy," wrote Paine. "Several died of the cold, or were choked by the sand which covered them after they fell exhausted."

Reefs off Cohasset rendered ships helpless for many years, at one time causing as many as forty wrecks in a nine-year period. Passages near Block Island and at Point Judith, Rhode Island, proved just as treacherous.[53] Rocks and ledges off the coast of Maine acquired colorful names, such as the reef near Great Cranberry Island, long called "Bunker's Whore" for the woman who drowned while rowing out to Captain Bunker's ship, and "Cold Arse," the ledge that juts out from Monhegan Island's shores, now called "Ragged Island."[54]

A striking personal account written by merchant John Brown to his son James in November 1782 shows that local traffic within Narragansett Bay was just as susceptible to unpredictable weather:

> *I returned from Carying Salley to Newport the Nite before Last we went from home Tuesday afternoone in the Packett[.] Caried Salley, Hopey and little Elcey with me[.] we stopt along side the Brigg Providence Capt Woodmon below the Crook hove up anchor and went both together to*

Bristol Harber with a moderate wind and Fair. The next day Wednesday at 10oclk in the morng[,] I sot off to Cary Salley & Hopey to Newport in the Packett with only Tom Walker beside them, & myself[,] the wind WSW and cold...the wind continued increasing till we got within 4 or 5 miles of Newport we took a double reef in the Mainsail, the wind blew harder and a grait sea rose[.] the Garles very sick...we could not take off the Bunnit off the Gibb for want of more help or of stoping the Tide strong against us and wind very high[.] we was off the Costed Harber at 3 in the afternoon when a sudden unexpected gust of wind& Rain took up and came much nearer oversetting the Packett than I ever did before or ever wish to again. Poor children[,] my heart aches to think of their Screeches[,] and for a few minutes I thought we was Gone. I happily got the Main Sheet and let it go with Difficulty[,] the Block being before split[,] I could not get it off Instantaneously and hollowed in vain to Tom to let go her Gibb Sheet[,] She being then on her Beam Ends and the water running in the Cabin Dores[.] he could not without Diving get at the Gibb Sheet just as soon as the Main sheet was gone she lifted[.] we then got down the Main sail and part of the Gibb and I put up the helm and run into Corringtons Cove and anchored and before nite made out to Get the Garles on shore.[55]

Perhaps the most well-known, or at least most oft-told, legend from these waters was the wreck of the *Princess Augusta,* sailing from Rotterdam to Philadelphia with a cargo of "Palatine" prisoners from Germany when it found itself "weakened by the death of half her hands [and] blown off her course" during a snowy gale in December 1720.

Nineteenth-century folklorists—most graphically, William P. Sheffield—would write that Block Islanders rushed down to the shore and murdered the crew and passengers for their belongings, though a cargo of prisoners seems an unlikely source of wealth. Islanders have always maintained that the crew abandoned the ship and passengers to their fate, setting it afire in the icy waters, a memorable sight, as the waves pulled the flaming ship toward the rocks and its demise.

In the years since that fateful night, the apparition of a burning ship that appears during the week between Christmas and the New Year has been sighted many times. An account by the Reverend S.T. Livermore in 1810 stated that "the light...is seen, sometimes one-half mile from shore, where it lights up the walls of a gentleman's rooms through the windows."[56]

A deposition taken from members of the crew days after the incident disclosed that the ship had suffered a great deal before it even reached the

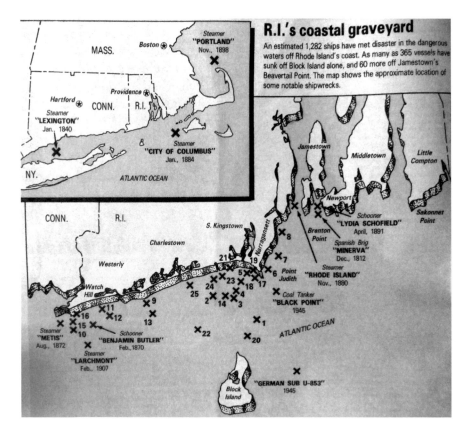

Map of "Rhode Island's Coastal Graveyard," *Providence Journal-Bulletin Sunday Magazine*, August 4, 1985. *Courtesy of Henry A.L. Brown.*

island. Provisions had become scarce, and half the crew had died. The remainder were "hobbled by the extreme cold." Captain Andrew Brook had encouraged the crew to save what provisions they could, "before and after she broke to pieces." The islanders maintained that they had rescued passengers and crew, and the fact that two sisters who survived lived among the islanders for many years after belies the rather ghoulish tale that popular publishers promoted. One sister married on the island and had numerous descendants who spent much of their lives attempting to tell the true story of the Palatine to journalists and later folklorists.

Before the installation of numerous beacons and lighthouses along the New England coastline, the passage around its many islands and shoals in rough weather relied solely on experience and luck, though a crew sometimes had help from those on land. In Marblehead, Massachusetts, in the early eighteenth century, a man named John Dimond, the grandfather of the later famous "seer" Molly Pitcher, was believed to be a wizard for, among other practices, his habit of venturing to the old burying ground on the hill overlooking the coast during a violent gale, "pacing up and down among the gravestones" and shouting orders "in a voice that could be heard even above the howling of the tempest…as if he were actually on the quarterdeck of the craft."[57] Strange as his behavior might seem, few doubted that it was his powers that guided ships safely past the deadly peninsula.

For the novice sailor, a storm at sea was a terrifying experience. Recordings of these experiences may be found among the many journals kept by sailors and passengers who survived life aboard an ocean-going vessel. The journal of the privateer *Yankee*, kept during a voyage in 1812 by captain's clerk Noah Jones, describes the weather often encountered off the coast in late October. Just ten days out of Bristol, Rhode Island, Jones wrote:

It is something singular that since we left port we have had only one pleasant day. There has been a continued succession of gales of wind from all parts of the compass, attended with torrents of rain, squalls, whirlwinds, thunder and lightening, and a tremendous sea frequently breaking on board and occasioning considerable damage; carrying away several spars and staving the arm-chests. Indeed it may be said that our vessel has sailed thus far under but not over the Atlantic ocean.[58]

In his *Incidents of a Whaling Voyage*, Francis Allen Olmstead recorded several occasions of the sudden appearance of a storm: "This evening we had a sharp squall, which we anticipated by taking in sail before it struck us. You see a light mist rising rapidly to windward of you, a signal to draw in your light sails, or in a few moments will be down upon you, screaming wildly through the rigging, while your light spars will be flying to leeward, or a topsail be blown with the sound of thunder from its bolt rope."[59]

During another voyage, around the Cape of Good Hope, he would experience a far more dangerous gale, writing, "Towards night, the wind hauled around to the South South West, and came in strong puffs, increasing into a gale by morning. The pitching and rolling of the ship, made my sleep very irregular, and as I held myself in my berth, the progress of the gale could easily be traced, not only by the roar of the wind growing louder, but also by the orders for taking in sail after sail."[60]

All ships caught in a gale were made to "lay to" with all the sails furled except for those deemed adequate by the captain to keep her bow

Detail from a watercolor by Frederic Roux showing the ship *Rubicon* of Boston during a storm three days out, on December 7, 1836. Reprinted in *Sailing Ships of New England,* Marine Research Society, 1924.

above the surge and prevent her from rolling windward, where the ship would be exposed to the sea's fury. Olmstead wrote of climbing up on deck early the next morning to find "the sea was lashed into foam, and breaking in broad white crests, from which the spray was blown like sleet in winter on shore."

After the experience of a gale at sea as a passenger on the brig *Jasper* en route to Malta in December 1832, Ralph Waldo Emerson wrote in his journal:

> *Last Ev'g fair wind and full moon suddenly lost in squall and rain. There are no attractions in the sailor's life. All the best things are alleviations. "A prison with the chance of being drowned."*[61] *It is even so and yet they do not run blind into danger as seems to the landman; those chances are all counted & weighed & experience has begotten this confidence in the proportioned strength of spars & rigging to the ordinary forces of wind & water which by being habitual constitutes the essence of a sailor's fearlessness...Storm, storm; ah we! The sea to us is but a lasting storm.*[62]

Such was the sailor's lot that even a captain, on occasion, would pity them, as did Captain William Driven, recalling a storm that engulfed his ship, the *Charles Doggett*, in January 1831. He said, "Our poor men, just out from home and fireside, miserably clothed, My God how they were suffering…Oh it was a fearful hour! One to try the soul of men. Could you have stood there on that groaning deck as we did, helpless and alone with God, you would have realized a scene which no pen could describe."[63]

Sailors' jargon contains expressions for these perilous situations. To "reach the end of one's rope" refers to the bruising task of "paying out" the anchor in rough weather only to find that you had reached "the bitter end" of the rope or chain secured to the deck with the anchor still dragging and not caught on the bottom. It was then you knew that the ship and crew were in danger of drifting with the current toward a rocky coastline. When bad weather came, sailors prayed that it came on open water.

Mariners logbooks and journals kept on vessels attest to the central role that weather played in a seaman's life while aboard; indeed, the wind, weather and seas are duly noted recurrently as conditions change through the day. The logbook of first mate Silvanus Crosby aboard the whaler *Asia* during 1791–92 is but one example. One entry reads: "Sunday March the 4th day 1792 first part of this 24 hours begins with fine weather the wind at ENE Steering by the wind…Calm later, a little dry rain just to puzel the dogs."

Crosby later described a particularly harrowing day and a half during a gale at sea: "July 6 Day 1792 First part of this day begins with Squally weather…Middle part the Sam latter part very rugged."

The next morning found the *Asia* in "rugged weather Wind at SSE Course WSW…Middle part very rugged Wind the same at 12 o'clock…Called all hands." The crew manned the vessel and guided the ship with "slack sale and run in under the lee of the land." With a telling palpable relief, the first mate ends his entry, "All hands well aboard the good ship Asia."

Later in the month came several days of "rough weather," and the more common, destructive element of enduring such squalls came to light—that of spoiling valuable foodstuffs in the hold: "Rain broke up our hold and brought up rum and bread and molasses." A later storm ruined supplies of beef and flour. Such loss of provisions could make for a long, hungry journey if another port was some distance away.

During the summer and autumn of 1746, Captain Benjamin Carr of Newport had cruised with his ship *The Duke of Marlborough* and achieved several "prizes," one of them being a Spanish snow loaded with timber and gunpowder. He dispatched a "prize crew" to bring it home, but by the middle of November, it had been run aground on Cape Cod, and the crew was forced to live on "dogs, rats and soaked hides for fifteen days."[64]

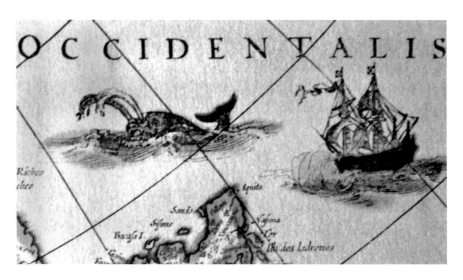

Whaling cartouche from a seventeenth-century map. *From the author's collection.*

Even when the relative safety of a port had been reached, an unexpected gale could cause calamity. Anchored in the port of New Providence in August 1741, the Rhode Island privateer *Revenge* found itself caught in a particularly violent thunderstorm: "At 9 PM it begun to thunder and Lightening very hard. Our Sloop Received great damage from a thunder bolt that stuckt our Mast and Shivered it very much, tore a large piece off the hounds and as it fell tore up the bitts[65] and broke in the hatchway, burst through both our Sides, and Started the plancks under her whale[66] melting several Cutlashes, pistolls, and fired off several Small Arms, the bullets of which stuck in her beam."[67]

Of all those who ventured on the sea, however, fishermen were most often at the mercy of the elements. Having smaller crews and smaller vessels to man meant that fishing boats were more vulnerable in storms than the larger vessels with which they shared the fishing grounds. In the Archives of Gloucester, Massachusetts, listings of those "lost at sea," we find grim testimony to the fate of many fishermen. As with merchant vessels, the hardscrabble fishermen who inhabited the coast often left a legacy of three or four generations of fishermen. At times, a family's legacy disappeared in a single tragedy as in the winter of 1720, when "Elias Babson, son of James was lost at sea with brothers John and Josiah…all James sons got their living by fishing."[68] Generations of fisherman later, brothers Freeman and Henry Abbot from Rockport suffered the same fate along with nine others aboard the *Yankee Girl* on September 8, 1869.

With the unpredictable weather prevalent along the New England coastline, even the everyday fishing excursion could turn treacherous. Dories were often swamped in rough surf, and men were known to fall overboard laying out trawls just offshore. A poem inscribed on a tombstone in Block Island's cemetery attests to a tragedy that locals knew all too well:

Not lost, but gone before
We miss thee dear Alfred wherever we go
Friends and relatives could not save
Thee from the raging wave
'the sea ran high when they were afloat
and hurled them from their little boat'
Capt. William A. Dunn Drown March 24, 1883 AE 23 years[69]

Local fishing vessels often fell prey to sudden storms. The patriotically named John Quincy Adams, son of Ezekiel and Nancy, was among the eleven who perished when the schooner *Forest* was lost on Chatham Beach while fishing for mackerel in October 1841. In times of severe storms, the impact could be devastating. On October 14, 1712, fishing crews were surprised by "a Sabbath-day storm on return from Cape Sable (Nova Scotia)…all crews of four vessels lost."[70]

In 1777, twenty-one-year-old Zerubbabel Allen Jr. was one of "a large co. of mostly Gloucester men lost at sea." The toll was said to be sixty men aboard the privateer *Gloucester,* under command of Captain John Clouson. Zerubbabel's namesake was a merchant seaman who had also been lost at sea in 1756, a mere three months or so before his birth.[71]

Celia Thaxter wrote of the year-round fishermen of the coastal islands in Maine:

They lead a life of the greatest hardship and exposure, during the winter especially, setting their trawls fifteen or twenty miles to the eastward of the islands, drawing them next day if the winds and waves will permit, and taking the fish to Portsmouth to sell. It is desperately hard work trawling at this season, with the bitter wind blowing in their teeth, and the flying spray freezing upon everything it touches,-boats, masts, sails, decks, clothes completely cased in ice, and fish frozen solid as soon as taken from the water.[72]

For those who ventured out fishing beyond New England's coast, scores found death in the gales found off Georges Banks, just as unlucky fishing

Fisherman's Memorial, Gloucester, Massachusetts. *From the author's collection.*

vessels still do today. A report of the sinking of the schooner *Jacob Bacon* in late February 1879 lamented the loss of the crew of twelve, "all active men in the very prime of life."

The same tragedies occurred in every community, as Henry David Thoreau found while wandering through the old town cemetery in Truro on Cape Cod in July 1855, when he came upon a monument that read:

> *Sacred*
> *to the memory of*
> *57 citizens of Truro,*
> *who were lost in seven*
> *vessels, which*
> *foundered at sea in*
> *the memorable gale*
> *of Oct. 3d, 1841.*

More common to the seaman than the recollection of the countless storms encountered were the permanent scars and disfigurements caused to the crew by the numerous accidents that occurred on board a ship. Perhaps the most common in the age of sail was as described in Crosby's log with this entry:

> *April the 29th day 1792*
> *Cabbin boy went up to help furl the mizintopsale and got up far as the top and went to make a grab at the top mast [lost] his hold and came down by the Lump which will Prove his fatte But we are in hopes of his recovery.*

Such misfortune—and often death—came to the inexperienced, or green hands, who had signed aboard ship. The sons of farmers, like John Barlow, wishing to escape the drudgery of farm work, were often called "grass combers" by the crew until they had their sea legs. Some never made it that far, such as the unfortunate sailor whose task was to haul a bucket of seawater to the deck and who fell overboard when the ship heaved starboard in a sudden swell.

Accidents on board ships were commonplace, even among experienced rovers, as manifested by the number of sailors who returned home crippled or deformed in some way. In his book *The Sea Rovers Practice*, historian Berenson Little wrote, "The men who died sea roving would number in the many thousands, and those crippled many times more."[73]

Scene in an East Boston shipyard. *From an engraving in* Gleeson's Pictorial.

The prevalence of missions and "Seaman's Houses" that grew in portside communities, especially in the nineteenth century, to support these men is a social history unto itself. Sailors away from the sea were often not only handicapped by whatever injury kept them ashore but also alcoholics and ultimately destitute, echoing what Barlow had foreseen.

An exception was Baranabas Downs, a naval seaman who enlisted at the beginning of the Revolutionary War and served in the seacoast companies of Captain James Davis and Captain Elisha Nye before joining the crew of the *Bunker Hill*, a privateer under command of Captain Isaac Cobb. The ship and its crew were captured six days out of port, and Downs was eventually freed by terms of an exchange of prisoners. He next joined the crew of the *General Arnold*, which was wrecked off the coast of Plymouth, Massachusetts, in December 1778 (see Chapter 5). Downs survived the wreck but lost both feet to frostbite and "ever after walked on his knees."

His neighbor in Barnstable noted, "He worked in his garden in pleasant weather, cut up wood, and did many jobs about his house. In the winter, and during unpleasant weather he coopered for his neighbors. He also cast spoons, ink stands, and other small articles, in pewter or lead, a business in which he exhibited some skill." Despite these admirable efforts, he was not self sufficient, and "a collection was annually taken up for his benefit by the church."[74] Such was the fate of many an ordinary seaman who survived an onboard catastrophe, but as Berenson Little indicates, a great number of men died on ship. Although no such known study has been conducted, it is safe to say that in every ships' log of every journey made during the age of sail, a death is likely to be recorded.

The causes of death were the same for many in the maritime trade but also often related to the type of vessel signed onto by the sailor. Naval vessels naturally took on an added risk in time of conflict, but we have seen that very few fatalities occurred aboard military ships during this period. Crews, whether enlisted or "consigned" to service, would have worked under a strict regiment and been the soberest of sailors in battle or heavy weather. Storms caused most fatalities on naval vessels, as the weight of guns and ammunition caused the vessel to lay lower in the water and increased the chances of a sailor being swept overboard in rough weather. The guns on deck or below could break loose and crush the gunner or another crew member. A fatal accident might also occur during the struggle to make the vessel less top heavy by lowering guns to the hold or, if in desperation, casting cannon over the side of the ship.

In the onset of a sudden gale, these duties and their performance in a timely fashion often meant life or death at sea. When two merchant schooners, the *Hamilton* and *Scourge,* were pressed into service for the American Navy during the War of 1812, they were re-outfitted and dispatched with heavy guns to Lake Ontario. It wasn't long before they encountered a British squadron, and a skirmish ensued with some damage to both vessels. That night, a sudden squall came up before repairs could be undertaken, and being top heavy on account of the guns, the foundering vessels were soon overwhelmed and taken to the bottom.[75]

Sailors aboard a merchant vessel in the eighteenth and nineteenth century faced the greatest risk from privateers. As compared with the "landsmen" aboard these ships, they had little in the way of defense, except perhaps pistols and cutlasses, and they were heavily outnumbered, especially if the privateer managed to get alongside and send its crew aboard.[76]

Merchant ships were lightly gunned as well. There is one record of a 170-ton vessel having "mounted only six old cannon probably firing three-pound shot...and a few small arms." As historian Benerson Little observed, "Merchantmen were manned by sailors, not privateers or men who went to sea to fight for plunder, an important distinction. And more important, merchantmen were cargo carriers first, fighting ships only by foul circumstance, and their decks often so cluttered with goods that anything under an hour was considered excellent for making a ship clear for engaging."[77]

Merchant ship sunk by privateers. *Courtesy of the Library of Congress.*

With this inequality on the high seas, colonial governors hired private men-of-war to patrol the coastline, but these often shied away from any exchange of cannon fire or skirmish on the high seas, often hightailing it back to harbor "without exchanging a single shot."[78] European nations created convoys of armed vessels to escort merchant ships, and ships of different nations would even sail together through treacherous waters under mutual agreement, though these were not always successful. The convoy protecting the merchant vessel might be outgunned by the pirate ships. And if the weather was becalmed as the convey kept windward, there was little the ships could do if a privateer sent out a boisterous and well-armed crew in longboats to board and plunder the "protected" vessels.

As a last resort, the crew of a merchant vessel could huddle in "closed quarters" and hope to stave off the attack until help came or the pirates gave

Pirates board a ship in this popular illustration from *Lost Ships and Lonely Seas*.

up. The captain could also decide to run the vessel ashore. A privateer was less likely to send longboats to board a grounded vessel, and the merchant crew could always burn the ship and abandon it before the pirates could board.

For the crew of a slave ship, the insurrection of the captives aboard was the greatest concern. Captains of slave ships were often fond of brutal punishments performed on deck before the other captives and crew, both to mete out discipline and to deter any thoughts of revolt among those in bondage. When insurrections did occur, they were violent and often viciously put down.

During Captain Peleg Clarke's journey from Providence at the beginning of the American Revolution, his crew began to fall ill, and the captives soon revolted. The crew managed to keep the ship but killed thirty-one of the slaves who rose against them. Almost every insurrection aboard a slave ship ended in similar circumstances until the revolt aboard the *Amistad* in April 1839, subsequent trial and popularity of which with the American public "gave enslaved rebels and their resistance a more important place in an expanded, radicalized movement against slavery."[79] Indeed, the publicity of the case and eventual success of the Mende men to gain freedom for their people may have inspired a spontaneous but ill-fated insurrection aboard the *Cassander*, a Providence whaling vessel that sailed from port on November 19, 1847.

According to accounts, Captain Winslow's crew was shorthanded, and they picked up two natives along the coast of Africa. Within some days, however, the two Africans became convinced that once in America, they would be bound over as slaves. Plotting their escape, they set fire to the ship on the early morning of May 1, 1848, and leapt overboard.

The vessel was soon engulfed in flames, and though the crew managed to climb aboard and lower a longboat, they were forced to leave with little in the way of possessions or provisions. They managed to pull one of the Africans into the boat, and he confessed the motive for the fire. The crew drifted for ten days without food before being picked up by a passing ship, during which time two people had died of starvation.[80]

Mutiny of a crew was also a concern with owners, especially those who sent out whaling vessels on journeys that could last as much as four or five years. The captains and mates of whaling vessels acquired a reputation for cruelty long before Melville's Ahab had entered the canon. As maritime historian Elmo Paul Hohman noted, "Impressed with the necessity of maintaining discipline through their own efforts, the captain and mates were commonly domineering and autocratic, often bullying and unreasonable, and upon occasion brutal and cruel."[81]

In 1840, seaman Frederick Jones stood accused with eight others of mutiny aboard the bark *Almira* during a four-year journey from New Bedford to around Cape Horn and back. Jones testified in the U.S. Commissions Court in Boston, "The captain had treated the crew rudely, abusing and keeping them at short allowance. The captain had struck Jones with a handspike, [and] the men did not have enough to eat, although there were plenty of provisions and water."[82]

Crew members believed they were being short-changed so that officers could earn some extra income by selling off provisions in ports of call. Another crew member testified that when he complained of a short allowance, "the (captain) said they would fare worse before he got through with them" and that "the captain and mate had struck, kicked, and choked him."

Finding that the captain and owner's written depositions did not defend such conduct, the court discharged the accused whalers. As common as the moniker of "Captain Death" might be among rovers, violence was not restricted to officers on a ship but also, especially on long journeys, often broke out among the crew. The captain of the bark *Atlantic*, also out of New

Whaling Ship, by John Sisson. *Courtesy of the Book and Tackle Shop, Westerly, Rhode Island.*

Bedford, would note the deaths during the cruise of 1865–68 on a separate piece of paper inserted in the log, including the notation of May 23, 1868, when "Jas. M. Foster was stabbed by the cook while leaning against a cask by the foreswifter…lived only about 5 minutes afterward."

Of the ships that plied the Atlantic during this period, signing aboard a whaling vessel would have been considered the most dangerous of marine occupations. Without question, the very nature of the endeavor made the likelihood of accident, injury and death far greater aboard a whaling vessel. Olmstead wrote that in the life of the whale man, "narrow escapes from death mark his career, and the ordinary dangers to which he is exposed, the prospect of which often blanches the cheek of the novice, have become familiar and are forgotten in the ardor of his exciting pursuit."

Amos C. Baker was the third mate aboard the *Ashawonks* during a voyage in 1864, when the crew spied two whales off the coast of Patagonia. Three boats were lowered, and the men rowed out to capture the pair. After the whales had been harpooned, Baker moved forward in the boat to finish the leviathan with the lance, and in the instant that he thrust it home, "the whale caught his boat with its tail, and the next thing Baker knew he was lying in a half of the boat, the other half having been reduced to splinters, and one of Baker's legs had been broken above the knee."

Above: Perils of whaling, as illustrated in *The Capture*, a lithograph made in 1862 by Endicott & R.S. Gifford. *Courtesy of the Book and Tackle Shop, Westerly, Rhode Island.*

Left: Postcard showing the sculpture *The Whaleman* by Bella Platt, New Bedford, Massachusetts. *From the author's collection.*

Such accidents were not uncommon as the whales struggled for their lives, at times coming up beneath a boat to send all the men tumbling into the deep. Most men who lost their lives in pursuit of a whale were taken unawares by the flying harpoon lines. As the whale sounded and "dragged out the line," a coil of rope often caught around a sailor's body or a limb and pulled him from the boat to be quickly dragged down. There are cases when this happened so suddenly in the heat of the struggle that the others didn't notice a crew member missing until it was over.[83] Sometimes the line caught in the crotch of the bow and carried the entire boat and crew underwater.

Perhaps the most arduous task aboard a whaling vessel was the process of "cutting in" the whale just taken. A rope or chain would be passed around the flukes and the whale towed to the bowsprit bits in the forward part of the ship. After the whale was secured with ropes and blocks, a staging was lowered for seamen to begin cutting the whale with lances and gaff hooks. The whale was "bled" by a deep incision and a large hole cut in which to place the "blubber hook," a task described by Francis Allen Olmstead: "To point the hook into the orifice made for it, one of the boatsteerer's having upon his feet a pair of woolen stockings to prevent his slipping, jumps overboard, guided buy a rope passing under his arms and tended by one of the men on deck." In this manner, the seaman had to secure the hook into the whale, "while the sea is dashing the whale against the ship and the waves are breaking over him; so that a man runs the risk of being strangled, or of being bruised by the concussion of the animal with the vessel."

Not to mention the sharks in the bloodied water below, just feet from the sailors, which mutilated many limbs or took a man to his death over the years of whale fishing.

Despite these often-horrific accidents, Olmstead considered a whaling vessel the safest ship to weather a storm for the sheer numbers of the crew:

> As far as safety is concerned, the preference most undoubtedly belongs to whale ships. In the American merchant service, a much less number of men are shipped to navigate…in a ship of 400 tons for instance, sixteen or seventeen men "all told" would be considered her complement, giving each watch seven men perhaps, whose duty is alternatively to take care of the ship. A whaler of this tonnage would carry over thirty men, giving to each watch double the force of the merchantmen.

Disease took the heaviest toll on the men confined to close quarters in a damp and often leaky vessel. Sailors knew that one should never sleep in wet clothes, but conditions on board, especially in a humid climate, often tossed old Atlantic axioms aside. The most common of these diseases were the ague, now known as malaria, and *le mal de Siam*, or yellow fever. Thousands fell to sickness, especially unseasoned sailors on their first, and often only voyage. Scurvy and other diseases due to dietary shortcomings were common as well, thus the serious risk brought about by losing valuable foodstuffs in a storm, as occurred on the *Asia*.

In some seasons, the entire Atlantic fleet suffered an epidemic of one devastating illness or another. Returning to Crosby's logbook for the *Asia*, we find that in early October, while anchored in New Providence, "The Doctor came of and noculated both our cruese for the Small Pox is so [great] that it is employable to keep clear of it—it is so [great] that 129 died in one day. There is one ship along side of us that has got 2 or 3 down with it."

Within a week, the captain also lay ill, and the doctor continued to visit the ship daily. The crew spent the days cleaning and re-cleaning the ship thoroughly, as well as going ashore for fresh supplies.

Many were not so fortunate to be in harbor during a wave of illness and often had to battle the elements as well as disease to bring the afflicted ship to the nearest port for treatment. American ships did not carry a surgeon aboard and instead relied upon the experience of the captain and mates to carry those duties when necessary, as well as the well-stocked chest of medicines and primitive instruments that were taken on every journey.

During Olmstead's voyage on the *North American*, he wrote of such a medical crisis at sea in the South Atlantic:

> *Tuesday Dec. 10*
> *Upon going on deck this morning after breakfast, we saw a ship upon our weather quarter standing towards us, and from her taking in sail, concluded that she was desirous of speaking with us; accordingly, we hauled our main topsail aback, awaiting the approach of the stranger.*

The ship was the *Messenger* of New Bedford, and as the ships passed, the captain hailed the crew of the *North American*, requesting that its captain come aboard to consult on the case of a mate who lay dangerously ill. Olmstead accompanied "Captain R" aboard the *Messenger*. The ship appeared to be clean and well kept, the journalist noted, as they were led to one of the state rooms where the sick man lay. Olmstead wrote, "He had been laboring under a violent fever for a long time, which had affected his mind, so that it was with some difficulty we were able to ascertain his exact state of feeling...

Capt. Kendrick of the *Messinger* said that he knew nothing of the treatment necessary, and requested that Capt. R prescribe whatever he thought proper."

Writing well into the first half of the nineteenth century, the novice mariner would note that he thought it "a wonder indeed, that sailors escape the effects of disease as often as they do, since they are out of reach of medical advice for so long a time. Every master of a vessel is the physician and surgeon aboard his ship; his medicines are all numbered corresponding to certain numbers in a little pamphlet of directions accompanying them and whenever necessary, he makes a selection according to the best of his judgement [*sic*]."[84]

Olmstead himself had not escaped illness earlier in the voyage and had written dishearteningly, "Undisturbed repose is out of the question, where everything is in motion and the bulkheads are dismally creaking. The air of the cabin of a ship is always close and uncomfortable in bad weather. Let man be sick anywhere else but on shipboard."[85]

The two vessels set course and "kept company" for a few days, with Captain R. paying visits to the ill mate who seemed to be improving. During this time, another ship, which had been spotted on the early morning of December 11, "came up and rounded to under our lee."

The ship was a whaling vessel, the *William and Eliza*, from New Bedford. Olmstead accompanied Captain R. as they were rowed in a longboat to visit both vessels though "the sea was very 'rugged,' and we mounted upon the ridges of the rolling billows and descended again, while the huge waves threatened to engulf us." On the *William and Eliza*, the captain had suffered a broken leg and desired Captain R.'s opinion on the progress of its healing.

The visitors stayed for some length of the day in the captain's "handsome cabin," and despite the prospects of a luxurious feast compared to the "salt junk" that had been their diet, they rowed back to the *North American*, as Captain R. was unwilling to remain any longer from his ship in rough weather.

This was common among the whalers, as Olmstead noted, "It is customary for the masters and officers of whalers, while cruising upon the same 'grounds,' to make frequent interchanges of visits. Towards evening the ships draw near to one another, to allow their officers an opportunity of having a 'gam,' which continues sometimes to a late hour."[86]

These "gams" or gatherings, where captains and mates could exchange news about the hunting grounds and other ships encountered, doubtless bolstered Olmstead's opinion of whalers' camaraderie and their manner of looking out for one another.

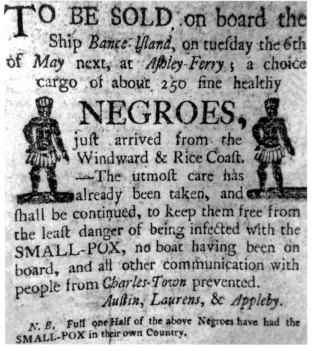

Above: Postcard of the fishing fleet, Gloucester, Massachusetts. *From the author's collection.*

Left: Advertisement for the sale of "a choice cargo" of slaves. *Courtesy of the Library of Congress.*

Among the merchant ships, however, there was little camaraderie on the open water or concern for the condition of the crew. Each captain of a merchant vessel was charged with getting goods quickly and efficiently from one port to another and so conducted the ship with sometimes-merciless affliction on the crew. Olmstead noted that crews on the whaling ships looked askance at merchant captains who took unnecessary risks, writing, "There are many ships, particularly merchantmen, that do not send down

their lofty spars, to ensure them against the risk of being carried away…
But to the sperm whaler, who is to be absent for several years from home,
and whose wanderings often lead him out of the reach of assistance, these
precautionary measures are the part of wisdom."[87]

It was not uncommon for ill-treated seamen to abandon ship once they
reached land or for the merchant captain to hire on a crew of seasoned
sailors and green hands when needed, in any port. Until the creation of
maritime courts after the American Revolution, mariners from New England
had little recourse in the way they were treated aboard ship, an island as it
were, considered by most ship owners and the majority of authorities as the
captain's domain.

Health was a more important concern aboard a slave ship. Vessels were
routinely scrubbed down with water and vinegar and the captive slaves
brought on deck for fresh air while the green hands among the crew cleaned
the shackle-laden hold. The crew of Captain Cyprien Sterry's slaver *Mary*,
out of Providence, was "employed tending the slaves every day; the slave's
quarters was given a major cleaning every two weeks."

When illness did occur, some captains took every measure to keep both
crew and human cargo healthy. When an outbreak of smallpox infected
Captain Samuel Chase's slaver after a stop in Mozambique in 1797, he spied
an uninhabited island and had the infected slaves rowed ashore, constructed
shelters and had the crew nurse them back to health for nearly a month with
large quantities of turtle soup.

Not every captain was as conscientious. When Rowland Robinson returned
to his home port with a cargo of slaves for the Narragansett Plantations,
even he reputedly was appalled at their condition. Local historian and poet
Caroline Hazard wrote of the shameful homecoming:

> *Most ghastly the sight*
> *when seen in the light*
> *of the sun that shone at mid-day.*
> *Weak, starving, and feeble, and quaking*
> *With fear,*
> *Naked, unable to stand*
> *Half-dead and wounded, and covered with filth*
> *The cargo was brought to the land.*

Hazard, like other historians before her, told of the "transformation" of
Rowland Robinson at the sight. He proclaimed it a sin and a shame, and

"his tears drowned the oaths that he swore." Robinson brought his share of twenty-eight slaves to his farm and nursed them back to health, even giving many their freedom. Rowland Robinson's story has been told and retold as an early example by local historians of how New Englanders "reformed" from their tolerance and even active participation in slavery during the colonial period, though it is difficult to reconcile the treatment of the slaves on his ship during the long journey with the remorse that Robinson showed once home.

For the experienced seaman, there would also be his personal log of "remarkable occurrences," those events on the water that he had experienced himself, or that he had heard secondhand in the interchange of stories and news from around the Atlantic world. Perhaps one of the most remarkable of these was the story of the vanished crew of the *Anna Verona*, a merchant ship out of Boston that was found drifting off the coast of Venezuela on August 23, 1821.

One of the large lifeboats was gone, but any supplies the crew might have taken remained on board. The ship's log was found to contain a shakily written entry from Captain Bennet Robinson dated August 17, when the crew encountered an unknown sea creature:

> *Ill omens continued to follow our crew. As night gave way to daybreak, Mr. O'Reilly shouted from the crow's nest that he had espied a mermaid with a comb and a mirror in her hand.*
>
> *The skies rolled red this morning, never auguring good, and it was half past the seventh bell that first we saw it—in the distance—rearing its head from the choppy waters, as a hungry dog would raise it over a tabletop, upon scenting a particularly aromatic leg of mutton. Its scales were greener than emeralds, its eyes an old and evil yellow, as of parchment left to cook in the sun. Its claws shone bright, as if cut from diamonds, and its tale [sic] thrashed as if possessed upon its own.*
>
> *How we were able to drive the monster back, I could not tell you. Many is the hour we fired the cannons, barely denting the beast's skin. We can only pray that we shall not again see its like afore we return to shore.*

The first reference to a sea serpent in America is by one Obadiah Turner, writing from Lynn, Massachusetts, in September 1641 that "some being on ye great beache…did spy a most wonderful serpent a shorte way off from ye shore. He was as big round in ye thickest part as a wine pipe; and they do affirme he was fifteen fathome of more in length…Wee have likewise heard yt at Cape Ann ye people have seene a monster like unto this which did there come out of the sea and coil himself upon the land." John Josselyn, in his *Account of Two Voyages to New England* (1674), mentions a similar story of "a sea serpent or snake that lay coiled on a rock."

In 1802, Reverend Abraham Cummings and family observed a sea serpent in the Gulf of Maine from their carriage on the coast road and recounted, "His head was rather large like a horse, but formed like that of a serpent. His body we judged was more than sixty feet in length. His head and as much of his body as we could discover was all of a blue colour except a black circle around his eye. His motion was at first moderate, but when he left us and proceeded towards the ocean, he moved with the greatest rapidity."[88] Author J. L. Homer would recall years later, "The sea serpent first made his appearance on our coast in 1817, which was the great year for seeing him. He moved about Boston Bay, in almost every direction, sticking chiefly to the North Shore, the waters near Cape Ann, Half Way Rock, Nahant, etc. Sharks and horse mackerel were constantly in attendance on his majesty. Bulletins in relation to him were issued from Gloucester during the travelling season, and published in the *Boston Gazette, Centinel* and *Palladium*, then the leading journals of the city."

In 1818, a written description was made of a creature spotted in the waters off of Nahant, Massachusetts: "His head appeared about three feet out of water, I counted thirteen bunches on his back—my family thought there were fifteen—he passed three times at moderate rate across the bay, but so fleet as to occasion a foam on the water…my family and myself judged that he was from fifty and not more than sixty feet in length."[89]

Paul Heuvelman, the foremost authority on the sightings of these creatures, wrote in *The Wake of the Sea Serpents* that in the period from 1817 to 1847, there occurred the most sightings, with sea serpents of the same descriptions appearing with regularity off the coast of Massachusetts and other locations along the Atlantic seaboard.

Such was the regularity of sightings—and so fresh in a mariner's memory did they stay—that unsurprisingly, such speculation of a similar creature was brought about in the wake of another mysterious occurrence in New England.

In May 1850, the residents of a fishing village near Brenton's Point in Newport, Rhode Island, spotted a familiar vessel on the horizon. It was the *Sea Bird*, a merchant vessel owned by Captain John Durham, a veteran seaman from Connecticut, and well known in Newport Harbor. Oddly,

Sea serpent spotted off Nahant, Massachusetts, in 1818. *Courtesy of Wickimedia.*

however, the ship sailed past the wharves, veering east and then north toward Easton's beach, where it ran aground on a sandbar close to shore.

A group of local fishermen immediately rowed out to the ship to see what had gone wrong. They found no one aboard, save a cat and a friendly dog, who led the astonished men about the boat. They discovered the mess table set for breakfast for the eight crew members, and reportedly, the coffee was still boiling on the stove. The crews' quarters smelled strongly of tobacco smoke, as if they'd only just finished a pipe and took a stroll on deck.

In the captain's cabin, all seemed normal. The navigational instruments were in place, and sixty dollars was on the captain's desk, assuring the men that the ship had not been a victim of piracy. The captain's log last entry read, "Branton Reef sighted," an indication that the entire crew had somehow disappeared within two miles of Newport. This was confirmed when another fishing vessel reported that it had sighted the *Sea Bird* on its way to Newport and had even hailed Captain Durham, who reportedly waved back from the deck.

The fishermen unloaded the vessel's holds of tropical hardwoods, pitch pine, sacks of coffee and dyewoods, goods from Honduras for which Newport merchants had been waiting, and tried every effort to refloat the ship, but the *Sea Bird* had ground deep into the sandbar.

While an inquiry began and speculation grew as to the reason for the crew's disappearance, a heavy gale came up one night, and waves pounded the shore and the sandbar where the *Sea Bird* still lay. When people came down to Easton's beach the next morning, they expected to find the ship a complete wreck, with its debris littering the shore. Instead, the ship had disappeared entirely, lifted up from the bar and taken out to sea.

On first sight of the empty ship and the remnants of the vanished crew, some local fishermen had mentioned that a sea monster might have taken the sailors. It seems that numerous sightings from reputable fishermen had taken place that year of a creature "larger than a whale slithering along the coast."[90]

No trace of any crew member or Captain Durham was ever found, and the *Sea Bird* was never seen again, leaving only an enduring mystery of Rhode Island lore.

CHAPTER 4

Death at Sea

In spite of those long-held rituals and practices to ensure the safety of the crew, a few deaths were inevitable on any seagoing voyage. When it came, the amount of ceremony attached to the ritual of burial at sea depended both on the type of vessel on which the sailor had expired, as well as the rank or standing of the deceased. As might be expected, the ritual was most formalized aboard a military vessel where the ceremony included "prayers for the dead," a brief supplication, followed by the ceremony of firing the guns. The *Seaman's Grammar* indicates that three volleys was common, though sometimes there was an exception. When the young brother of Captain Phillips aboard the *Hannibal* died, he was committed to the deep with "prayer, drums and trumpets, and sixteen guns, one for each year of his life."[91]

Ceremonies for captains and mates would have been more elaborate, and special care was taken whenever possible to give such persons "a Christian burial" on land. First mate J.D. Purdee wrote from the *Eunice H. Adams* to its owner on February 27, 1885, "It becomes my painful duty to inform you that Captain Marchant died at 5:45 p.m. yesterday. Up to Sunday night he was apparently better than without when we arrived here, but an accuit attack of Brane trouble set in and he sank very rapidly for the last two days of his illness."[92]

Officers of the ship were buried in custom-made, weighted coffins. The ship's flag would be lowered to half-mast, and "bigger guns, often the greatest cannon were fired to solemnize the occasion."[93]

Privateer crews would hold an equally respectful ceremony, and as Benerson Little writes, "Rovers generally treated their dead with great respect; buccaneers gave them 'according to custom' a volley."[94]

Aboard a merchant vessel, the ceremony would have been brief and marked by its simplicity. The captain would serve to offer the supplication, a few of the crew might also offer testimony to the sailors work ethic or temperament and then the body would be committed to the deep, or "given the deep six," in sailor's jargon. The ritual of burial at sea could not be conducted until the ship had reached water six fathoms deep.

If the sailor had the misfortune of working a slave vessel and dying on board, his body was likely unceremoniously cast over after dark so that the cargo of slaves would not know that the crew who dominated them had been weakened.

For the ordinary seaman upon any vessel, death could come at any moment. "Even in calm seas," Marcus Rediker wrote, "the sailor could not escape reminders of his own mortality."

Much as any sailor might desire a secure burial place, Rediker wrote, "this most basic desire was contradicted by the central reality of work at sea. Land was usually nowhere to be found." Thousands of young men during the age of sail were "flungge over board" into "a grave wide and big enough" in what many sailors found a most undignified end.

Every rover, Jack Cremer noted, had interest in buying "a good hammock, or coffin you may call it, for (at sea) they always bury their dead in their hammocks." If a seaman's hammock was "ill used," the sail-maker was commissioned to make a shroud and sew the body inside, the last stitch made through the nose to be certain the sailor was deceased.

If the ship could spare the shot or ballast, some would be sewn into the hammock to facilitate a swifter fall to the bottom. Sharks were always a concern, and more than one sailor noted that despite all due ceremony, their departed shipmates were simply "meat for the fishes of the sea." One seaman, Frank Rogers, wrote that the day after the ship's cook had died and was sewn in a blanket and heaved overboard, "10 or 12 sharks hankered about the ship for another such meal."[95]

Rediker noted a ritual held several days after the burial among shipmates, when "the dead man's goods—his chest, bedding clothes, and the few other items he possessed, perhaps a book or two, cards or a musical instrument— were auctioned off as everyone gathered around the mainmast."

Shipmates paid "an extreme dear rate" for these items as a way to provide support for the family—a measure of generosity that was both indicative

A Ship in Distress. Illustration from *Lost Ships and Lonely Seas.*

of the bond and the brotherhood that seamen felt toward one another but also, as the historian assesses, "seamen sought to give value to a life that after years of toil had found no better end than a death in the middle of nowhere and an unceremonious burial in the briny deep."[96]

In the daily life aboard a ship, any formal remembrance was, of necessity, very brief. In the "wooden world" within which these sailors traveled, stories and songs of loss at sea would have been integrated gradually within the more traditionally known tales and ballads. As folklorist Duncan Emrich wrote:

> *With the work done, men relaxed in the forecastle and there (on occasion at least) sang songs unrelated to their work…These songs might be of any kind—ballads of love and disaster, hymns, sea-songs, the popular tunes of the day. A forecastle song might be sung by one man or by a few, or the entire group, depending upon the song. Those songs, as the one below, that dealt with death were sung as a remembrance of not only those long ago victims in the song, but also for those nearer to the able-bodied seaman and even their own experience.*

One forecastle song describes a sea disaster that took place in Maine at an unknown date. It was among the collection of songs recorded by Mrs. Carrie Grover of Gorham, Maine, for the Library of Congress in the early twentieth century.

Tis of a sad and dismal story
That happened off that fatal rock,
Where the New Columbia in all her Glory,
How she received that fatal shock.

We sailed from England in December,
From Liverpool the eighteenth day,
And many hardships we endured
While coming to America.

Two passengers from Pence came with Us,
Two brothers were from Birmingham,
They took the leave of all their people
To settle in New Eng-e-land.

We anchored in four fathoms water,
Thinking all our lives to save,
But 'twas in vain for shortly after—
Poor souls they met a watery grave.

Our ship she dragged away her anchor,
And on a rock, she split in two,
And out of eighty brave young seamen,
They all were lost, excepting two.

The song describes the grisly aftermath of the wreck along the shore. The bodies were "all taken and decently buried," and the song ends with a hymn-like incantation:

May God protect all absent seamen,
While plowing o'er the distant main,
And keep them clear from rocks and danger,
And safe return them home again.

May God protect all absent seamen,
The mother- and the fatherless,
And send his blessing on those poor people
Who have lost their sons in such distress.

Mariners' belief in an afterlife has always been somewhat murky—the tales of "Davey Jones's Locker" notwithstanding, a long-hewn tradition that threaded its way from the ancient "Jonah's locker" into the fabric of nautical folklore. By the eighteenth century, only those who had fallen overboard were destined for the locker, and a kind of heaven beneath the sea, called "Fiddlers Green," had been adapted from Irish folklore. It was here that "winsome, willing wenches danced to merry fiddlers tunes while grog and beer flowed freely from bottomless jugs."

As Marcus Rediker would write: "Little is known about the specific religious beliefs of seamen. Their thoughts about the body and the soul, salvation, sin, and the nature of heaven and hell have not been preserved. Yet formal religious affiliations among seamen were many, ranging from Catholic to Protestant, from the Church of England to Presbyterianism and Quakerism. Almost every denomination was represented. African, Asian, and native American seamen extended the range of religious belief."[97]

American mariners, as might be expected, came to be a more openly religious breed compared to their worldly counterparts. Their faith, deeply imbued in both ritual and purpose within daily life, gave them an expectation of returning home, of one day "hanging up the oars" and retiring to the land, where they could farm and live to a ripe old age. Any mariner would have envied the end of retired sea captain James Updike of Narragansett, who at the age of seventy-one, had gone "in a small boat alone a fishing, being gone two days, [the] boat was [then] found on [the] backside of Coananicut and he in it dead. 'Tis supposed he fainted and so died, suddenly; for he had rolled up his line, and everything on board seemed as tho he had done and was returning home."[98]

CHAPTER 5

Remembrance

The first act of remembrance, if you will, of a death at sea would have been the entry in the ship's log, traditionally marked by a crudely drawn skull and bones in the margin. These entries, as with other events, are often tersely drawn sentences on the page that leave little impression of the effect of death beyond a line in a maritime ledger and the death duly recorded in the custom house upon the ship's return. The record of the whaler *Zone* on its return to New Bedford on February 12, 1830, reads simply, "Built in Rochester 1827; lost first mate Nicholas Easton." At times, however, a first mate would record a memorial of a kind in just a few lines on the logbook's page. On the privateer *Yankee*'s return to Newport on March 12, 1813, after 146 days at sea, captain's clerk Noah Jones wrote:

> *It is with deep regret we mention the death of Mr. Jackson, late first Mate of the English Brig* Shannon, *who died at ½ past 12 midnight in great agony. Mr. Jackson, as before stated, was severely wounded by a cannon ball in the foot during a skirmish between the* Yankee *and the* Shannon *on the 24ᵗʰ ult. Notwithstanding every medical assistance, and all possible attention his wound terminated in the lockjaw, spasms, and death. Mr. Jackson belonged to Workington, was 23 years old, very much beloved by his captain and crew, and appeared to be a most excellent young man.*[99]

Once word of a disaster reached shore, newspapers would have spread the story throughout the immediate community and beyond as stagecoaches took news to destinations north and west. Newspapers routinely reported on the loss of ships at sea, though the information might be scant. Captains and merchants lost were often subject to some biography, but crews lost were only sporadically listed.

In many cases, memorial poems, pamphlets and broadsheets were printed for those lost at sea. Again, prominent captains were often the subject of these memorials, as evidenced by the poem printed "In Memory of Capt. John Crawford, of Providence who sailed on a voyage to the West Indies Dec. 11, 1746, and was lost at sea." A broadsheet printed in East Lyme, Connecticut, in 1872 of the "Lines Written in Memory of Capt. John Chapman Who it is Supposed was Lost At Sea Oct. 12, 1871" is a fair example of these tributes in verse:

They tell us of the Captain
who on an autumn day;
Did launch his little yawl boat;
set sail, and went away.

And so before the hurrying winds;
his noble vessel flew
Away to yonder fishing grounds;
He bade his home adieu.

Out there he spoke a friend who says
that "he was bound off shore"
The "Friend" returned to tell the tale
but the Captain came no more.

The loved ones he has left behind
say "Oh! How can this be;
That the Captain is now sleeping
midst the corals of the sea."

No bell was tolled, no sexton there
to see that "all was well,"
But the combers of the mighty deep
must "toll his funeral knell."

His friends, which like the countless sands,
that belt the ocean's shore;
All long again to welcome him,
but they'll see his face no more.

The tribute continues to intone the virtues of a pious man who took his children to church so that they might learn of "Jesus' tender care" and repeats the oft-told biblical tale of salvation before returning to the captain's fate:

...But oh, we should not wish him back;
He was prepared to go,
The ocean wave must be his grave
For God hath ordered so.

The bark that bore him swift away,
upon the ocean's wave;
Her bow had ploughed the mighty deep
and there should be her grave.

Through many a storm of rain and sleet,
and many an autumn's blast,
she lived and brought her captain home;
but this time was her last.

He has left this world of sorrow,
and his troubles here are o'er,
For he's anchored in that harbor,
where they never drag ashore.

These tributes and memorials printed on paper became keepsakes for family and friends and were an impermanent but effective method of preserving the memory of the individual within his community. One remarkable example is that of the "Ode...composed on the Death of a Young Man, who was Supposed to be Lost in a Storm at Sea, at the Request of his Sister by a *Female Friend.*" Printed in a Hartford newspaper in 1810, the poet asks for divine inspiration in communicating the grief of friends and asks in the fifth of thirty-two stanzas:

How must the tender parents['] heart,
with anxious care feel keenest smart,
to have their lovely son depart,
to sail the raging main;
And how must brothers kind and dear,
and sisters feel a grief severe,
and bid adieu with trembling fear
he'll ne'er return again.

In stanzas eight through ten, we learn of the young man's fate, a not uncommon occurrence in the shipping lanes during winter:

In January, the twelfth day,
in eighteen hundred ten, they say
they hoisted sail, and went away
to some far distant lands.
Soon did the blackening clouds arise,
and quickly overspread the skies
the raging storm excites surprise,
and we are led to fear,
their vessel tossed to and fro,
now rising high, now sinking low,
soon met a fatal overthrow;
for last of the we hear;

Is that a vessel sailing near,
viewed them in great distress appear,
light'ning their freight, with deep felt fear,
of overwhelming woe.
Alas the thought of such a state!
To see before us sudden fate,
no friends or woe can mitigate,
or kind relief bestow.[100]

In the event of a great catastrophe on their shore, the shared memories that became those oral and then printed histories reverberated through the generations, and these sites of disaster or another designated site were often memorialized long after those who had survived the event were gone.

Postcard of Highland Light, Cape Cod. *From the author's collection.*

One such disaster occurred off the coast of Plymouth on Christmas Eve 1778. Earlier that day, the heavily armed brig *General Arnold* had departed Boston in company with the ship *Revenge*, and it wasn't long before both captains realized they were sailing straight into the teeth of a snowy gale. The captain of the *Revenge* had the good fortune of a faster vessel and raced around the arm of the Cape, escaping the brunt of the gale and leaving the *General Arnold* behind, where Captain James Garnet ordered it anchored in hopes of safety off Gurnet Light.

The sails were furled and secured, and the crew lowered sixteen of the twenty guns into the hold and then bunkered in the cabin to wait out the storm. By midnight, the gale was at such a fury that the crew could feel the ship trembling with the battering of the waves, and when the ship's anchor began to drag, they realized their greatest fear with the certainty of being run aground. The captain ordered the last rations of rum to be distributed to the men, and they began to prepare themselves for the worst.

The helpless crew of the *General Arnold* endured the storm until the next day, when it abated near sunset, but then came the cold, and through that night, as the restless seas from the storm continued to batter the vessel, a number of the crew froze to death on the deck, having had to scramble above the flooded cabin.

Though mariners at Plymouth had spotted the stricken vessel lying half exposed on the white flats as the tide receded, they could not reach the vessel through the half-frozen harbor. Dories that were sent out for rescue could not get through the ice floes, and on Sunday, a number of volunteers began cutting a causeway through the ice to reach the wreck. When the men from Plymouth finally reached the ship on Monday morning, more than half of the crew had already died, and the handful of survivors were brought back to Plymouth houses and immersed in cold-water baths until they were revived. Captain James Garnet was among the survivors and attributed his life to having poured his ration of rum down his boots in the storm.

Another survivor, Barnabas Downs, wrote of those hours after rescue, saying, "I was carried to Mr. Bartlet's tavern whose kindness to me I would thus publickly acknowledge…My cloaths were first cut off from me and I was put in cold water in order to take out the frost: I was then placed in bed and having my teeth forced open had some cordials poured down my throat, but I have no remembrance of these transactions, for I lay perfectly senseless until 2 o'clock on Monday."[101]

The seventy-two casualties of the sinking of the *General Arnold* were first thawed in the Weir River and then placed in coffins and buried in a mass grave in the Old Burying Ground after a solemn funeral at the courthouse. Many of the sailors who died were from Cape Cod, and word did not reach their communities until several days after the funeral. The *Boston Gazette* did not publish an account of the tragedy until January 4, 1779.

A full seventy-four years after the tragedy, the naval heroes of the *General Arnold* were memorialized with a white obelisk on the site of their entombment above the harbor.

On occasion, the story of a disaster was lifted from the newspapers to the heights of poetry and thus the victims memorialized in a more permanent way. Such remembrance has a long history, extending back in song and oral histories that led to *The Odyssey*, the second stanza of which brings the reader at once into the life of a mariner at sea:

> *He saw the townlands*
> *and learned the minds of many distant men,*
> *and weathered many bitter nights and days*
> *in his deep heart at sea, while he fought only*
> *to save his life, to bring his shipmates home.*[102]

Monument to the men of the brig *General Arnold*, Burial Hill, Plymouth, Massachusetts. *Photo courtesy of the author.*

In America, these tragedies in verse echoed popular English poetic works, such as William Falconer's *The Shipwreck* (1760), which declared itself early on, in his three-canto telling of the sinking of the *Britannia*, that this is a tale of a different measure from those of the heroes of Empire:

> *No pomp of battle swells earths strain*
> *nor gleaming arms ring dreadful on the plain:*
> *But o'er the scene while pale remembrance weeps,*
> *Fate with full triumph rides upon the deep.*

Illustration of the British bark *Vernon,* shipwrecked on the beach in Lynn, Massachusetts, on February 1, 1859. *From* American Sailing Ships in New England.

As historian John R. Gillis observed, "In the nineteenth century, shipwreck became the symbol of the power of nature and the hopelessness of human efforts to control one's own fate on either land or sea."[103]

One of the first American poetic narratives of a shipwreck was written by Henry Wadsworth Longfellow, whose *Wreck of the Hesperus* (1840) was based on the sinking of the schooner *Favorite,* out of Wiscaiset, Maine. In December 1839, the ship had run aground in a storm on the rocks and reef of "Norman's Woe," a short distance from the westernmost point of Gloucester Harbor. In the aftermath of the wreck, twenty bodies washed ashore, including that of an older woman tied to a piece of the mainmast.

With poetic license, Longfellow changed the name of the ship to the *Hesperus,* after a well-publicized shipwreck near Boston, and changed the passengers on the doomed ship to an old salt and his daughter, whom he ties to the mast to ride the storm through the night:

> *At daybreak, on the bleak sea-beach,*
> *A fisherman stood aghast,*
> *To see the form of a maiden fair,*
> *Lashed close to a drifting mast.*

The salt sea was frozen on her breast,
The salt tears in her eyes;
And he saw her hair, like the brown sea-weed,
On the billows fall and rise.
Such was the wreck of the Hesperus,
In the midnight and the snow!
Christ save us from a death like this,
On the reef of Norman's Woe!

By the later nineteenth century, poets like John Greenleaf Whittier and Gerald Manley Hopkins were contributing to the literary canon and the growing mythology of the American mariner. New Englanders were almost always portrayed as indifferent to the suffering of the shipwrecked cast upon their shores; indeed, in story and verse there were accusations that "wreckers" lived along the coast who would lure ships to the rocks for their bounty. Theodore Fielder recorded that in researching the old story of the *Palatine*, he came upon an old farmer who had a recollection of the practice from long ago. He reported, "They tied a lantern to a horse's tail and whipped the horse around a haystack. The lantern looked as if she hung in the rigging of a ship in a rough sea. Any ship that saw the light would take the same course and come ashore. They always came ashore where they'd go to pieces quickly."

The legend was wrought into dramatic verse by John Greenleaf Whittier in 1867. Writing in the present at the start of the poem, Whittier introduces the reader to

that lonely Island fair;…
the pale health-seeker findeth there
the wine of life in its pleasant air.

But despite this description of a newfound paradise for Victorian vacationers, Whittier's poem calls back to a darker past on the island:

Opposite, top: Illustration from Whittier's *Ballads of New England* depicting a boat in distress off Marblehead, Massachusetts.

Opposite, bottom: Illustration of the women of Marblehead's punishment of Floyd Ireson, from Whittier's *Ballads of New England*.

The ship that, a hundred years before
freighted deep with its goodly store,
in the gales of the equinox went ashore.
The eager Islanders one by one
Counted the shots of her signal gun,
And heard the crash when she drove right on!
Into the teeth of death she sped
(may God forgive the hands that fed
the false lights o'er the rocky Head)
...down swooped the wreckers like birds of prey
tearing the heart of the ship away,
and the dead had never a word to say. [104]

Whittier became famous for his verses depicting New England landscapes and people, and like other poets of the period, he often transposed real-life events into dramatic verse. That this Quaker poet and ardent abolitionist saw native New Englanders as darkly mysterious and even evil-spirited is not unique to his literary imagining. It was a view that many intellectuals and artists shared at the time, including novelist Nathanial Hawthorne and author Edgar Allen Poe, and even Thoreau was put off by the locals collecting seaweed as the dead were taken from the beach after the wreck of the *St. John.*

But as John Gillis explains in *The Human Shore,* "This was not for any lack of sympathy, but reflected a different, older maritime sensibility that accepted death at sea as inevitable...shipwreck had a different meaning when sinkings were part of the natural order of things, something that should not give pause to the work of those whose fate was to die as well as live by the sea."

It is also telling, perhaps, that these writers were penning these portraits during a period when they and other "out of towners" were much disliked by those being displaced from their communities by entrepreneurs who sought to turn them into retreats for wealthy vacationers. Little surprise then, that those native New Englanders might have seemed standoffish to their overtures.

Whittier liked to explore and recount the mythology of this old New England in his poetry and seemed to especially relish those tales of hardscrabble justice meted out by the region's citizens.

In his collection *Ballads of New England,* the poet recounts such stories as that of Captain Floyd Ireson, who abandoned his leaking ship "with his own towns people on her deck!" On his return alone, after a night when every

mother and sister, wife and maid,
Looked from the rocks of Marblehead
Over the moaning and rainy sea,
Looked for the coming, that might not be

the women of the town administered their own trial and punishment.
In Whittier's famous *Skipper Ireson's Ride,*

Scores of women, old and young,
Strong of muscle, and glib of tongue,
Pushed and pulled up the rocky lane,
Shouting and singing the shrill refrain:
  "Here's Flud Oirson, for his horrid horrt,
Torr'd and futherr'dan'corr'd in a corrt
By the women o' Morble'ead."[105]

The poet, in particular, liked to tap that dark vein that tied New England women, especially widows and spinsters, to the practice of witchcraft. In *The Wreck of Rivermore,* another shipwreck narrative, the native superstitions and the dark consequences of dismissing them become central to the telling:

"Fie on the witch" cried a merry girl,
as they rounded the Point where Goody Cole
Sat by her door with her wheel atwirl,
  A bent and blear-eyed poor old soul,
"oho" she muttered, "ye're brave to-day!
But I hear the little waves laugh and say,
'The broth will be cold that waits at home;
For it's one to go, but another to come."

The seasoned captain warns the girl:

She's cursed...speak her fair:
I'm scary always to see her shake
Her wicked head, with its wild gray hair,
And nose like a hawk, and eyes like a snake.

When the boat becomes caught in a thick fog, "shot by the lightenings through and through," the crew veers and tacks back toward home, but the weather grows worse, and then "like a flail," the gale sends a wave that capsizes the boat. The wave coming ashore catches the attention of the "witch":

> Goody Cole looked out from her door:
> The Isles of Shoals were drowned and gone…
> She clasped her hands with a grip of pain,
> The tear on her cheek was not of rain:
> "They are lost," she muttered, "boat and crew!
> Lord, forgive me! My words were true!"

Herman Melville also added to the American canon from his own unique perspective—that of the seaman. As a poet, he was most famous for his religious and Civil War ballads, though as might be expected of the author of *Moby Dick* and other novels, he did turn occasionally to the sea. One example most striking is with his poetic narrative of the life of John Marr. When Marr settles down and marries, years later, even after children are born, he still finds himself yearning for the camaraderie, the "affections of the past" he shared with shipmates, though that is tempered in his thoughts by the reality of life on the sea:

> Whither, whither merchant sailors,
> witherward now in roaring gales?
> Competing still, ye huntsman whalers,
> in leviathan's wake what boat prevails?
> And man-of-war's men, whereaway?
> If no dinned drum beat to quarters
> On the wilds of midnights waters—
> Foremen looming through the spray;
> Do yet your gangway lanterns, streaming,
> Vainly strive to pierce below,
> When, tilted from the slant plank gleaming,
> A brother you see to darkness go.

Illustrations and paintings also used shipwrecks as a dramatic theme in romanticized European landscapes by Turner, de Marseille, Delacroix and Vernet, among others. By the eighteenth century, the "shipwreck painting" had acquired a formula of storytelling motifs, including "raging winds and waters, rocky abutments and outcroppings into the water, a wrecked and

Illustration of a boy lobstering above an old wreck from *Life Along the New England Shore.*

sinking ship, the stranded, desperate passengers scrambling across lifelines to a rocky shore, or huddled on-ship hoping for rescue, witnesses on far rock outcroppings watching the disaster and heroic male rescuers."[106]

American paintings depicted more realistic scenes than those dramatic renderings. Edward Moran's *Shipwreck* shows survivors wandering the shore while the ship lies foundered against the rocks just yards away.

Winslow Homer's famous *The Life Line* portrayed early rescue efforts. The stark image of a rescuer belaying a shipwreck victim just feet above the waves was based on the efforts to rescue passengers aboard the White Star Line's RMS *Atlantic* in 1873. Xanthus Russel Smith even created a pastoral scene, with a trio of old salts resting amid the remains of a long-decayed shipwreck.

This imagining of New Englanders in popular literature and art was quickly adapted as a kind of mythology, not only by readers in faraway places but also by New Englanders themselves. Commons and formal greens appeared where so long had been lonely fields by the meetinghouses. Sites of remembrance were marked out with memorials or cast-iron plaques at the scenes of battles or shipwrecks. Historical groups organized tours in New England towns. Great houses were saved from the wrecking ball, and preservation groups began to form in many communities.

CHAPTER 6
Living Alongside the Sea

Port towns and villages along the New England coastline had always held an intimate kinship with the sea, not only with the rocks, the sandy beaches and marshlands reached by the tide each day, but also with the great Atlantic beyond. There were so many men gone and not returned through the generations, but there was so much gathered and so many livelihoods sustained for generations, as well, until our own time. Like Morison's quote of God giving the sea to early New England settlers, there is also the familiar story of the Nantucket Islanders who trudged up the dunes to Folly's Hill overlooking the coast, and one, pointing out to a school of whales, proclaimed, "There is a pasture where our children's grandchildren will go for bread."

Starbuck relates in his Nantucket history that the remark was made in 1690, and within a decade, the whaling industry had taken hold under the guidance of Ichabod Paddock, a Cape Cod native who was hired to come to the island and whose people were known to have "a greater proficiency in the art of whale catching than themselves."[107]

For those who lived in such communities, the sea affected their everyday lives. If a family did not have at least one member at sea, it had members who worked in some capacity to support seagoing ventures and the mariners who undertook them. Rope manufacturers, sail makers, candle works and shops of carpenters and coopers, along with forges, shipyards, taverns and inns all thrived in such communities.

Postcard of New Bedford Harbor. *From the author's collection.*

And then there were the challenges and dangers wrought by the sea each year: the gales of spring, lightning storms in summer, the "Nor'-easters" of autumn and the ice storms during the long winters.

Young minister John Comer, of Boston, came to Newport at the age of twenty-one to serve as co-pastor of the First Baptist Church, where he stayed in that position for six years. Looking through the events of just one year in his diary, we find a glimpse of what these communities witnessed:

> *Mond., 13 (Oct. 1727) This day A.M. a boat was set over at Point Juda* [Judith] *with 4 persons on board. There being another boat in company we cold not help them, but soon got to town and inform'd, and with utmost speed a sloop went out and about 8 of ye clock in ye evening found them lying on ye side of ye boat with the sea washing over* [them], *having lain 7 or eight hours, and notwithstanding ye coldness of ye season and ye extreme difficulties they were exposed to, thro God's goodness all were brought safe to town.*[108]

Some months later, in early spring, survivors of a shipwreck were not so fortunate:

> *Lord's D. 7 (April 1728) This evening a schooner from ye Bay under ye command of Capt. James Emmit in a mighty storm of wind accompanied*

with rain and cast on shore, on a sand beach at Westport…and all got on shore, being 6 in number (save one Indian girl who was drowned in ye vessel); there were 4 Englishmen and one Indian. The 4 were so far spent with ye difficulties of ye storm, after they had traveled some distance from ye wreck [that they] dropt down dead a little space from each other. Ye Indian traveled a great part of ye night till he found a hay stack under which he sheltered till day, and [then] gave information so [that] they were all taken up and decently buried.

In October of that year, Newporters learned the news that "a sloop commanded by Wm Gardner with whom were Stephen and David Mumford, Peter Arault (Ayrault), and two Negroes was lost as is supposed by a sudden storm of snow (that) arose. They went to receive prohibited goods from Holland, but did not do it." The following spring, Comer learned a "remarkable relation from Capt. Robert Gardner's own mouth" concerning a sloop that the captain had sailed from Newport the previous September, bound for Antigua.

It seems that one night during the voyage, Gardner was "waked out of sleep 5 or 6 times from an uncommon dream of seeing strong men [yet] were so broken [that] he could scarce understand [them] &c., which so affected him [that] he got upon deck under great concern of mind not knowing [what] it should mean. Unbeknownst to the captain, the helmsmen had veered just slightly off course, and when he came up beleaguered in the morning…he espied about a league distant something floating on the water."

As the sloop grew closer, they could see that they were viewing a group of men holding up a sail on the upraised bow of a ship. This was a sloop from New Haven, Connecticut, that had also journeyed to Antigua but was caught in a sudden gale, with "the wind…blowing excessive hard, and ye sails furl'd, scudding before it; ye vessel ship't a sea which carried all upon deck over."

A "great sea"[109] had carried eight men off the deck initially, breaking the mast midway and damaging the waist of the vessel, carrying off the quarterdeck and breaking the bulkhead of the cabin. Some of those who scrambled out onto the deck were washed away by a second wave. Finding the stern rapidly sinking, the survivors made their way with great difficulty to the head of the ship. There they had lain for seventeen days, salvaging two hogsheads of water from the hold and surviving in part on sheep that had washed overboard and swum back to the vessel, as well as a dolphin that became trapped by swimming into the half-submerged ship.

Disaster at Sea. Illustration from *Ocean Steamships* (London: John Murray, 1892).

Illustration of Caswell's Peak, Star Island in the Isles of Shoals. Excerpted from *Picturesque America* (1870). *From the author's collection.*

Shipwrecks and "remarkable occurrences" were more common events in many seaside communities than those few published, purple-prose testimonies might lead readers to believe. In the aftermath of the famous wreck of the brig *St. John* off Cohasset in 1849, traveler Henry David Thoreau witnessed the mass burial plot dug for the 145 victims and the rough-hewn coffins stacked for the undertaker's wagons, and he even peered at the "many marbled feet and matted heads" of the dead as they waited to be identified. He philosophized that as an outsider, he could argue, "If this was the law of nature, why waste any time in awe or pity?"

However, he also acknowledged, "The inhabitants would be not a little affected by this event. They would watch there many days and nights for the sea to give up its dead, and their imaginations and sympathies would supply the place of mourners far away, who as yet knew not of the wreck."[110]

A quarter century later, poet Celia Thaxter wrote of walking the beach on an island after a storm in her memoir *Among the Isle of Shoals*. She said, "The driftwood is full of suggestions: a broken oar; a bit of spar with a ragged end of rope-yarn attached; a section of a mast hurridly chopped, telling of a tragedy too well known on the awful sea."[111]

Thaxter wrote that a disaster of sixty years before still reverberated among the collected memory of the islanders, that being the wreck, as is written in the records, of the "Ship Sagunto stranded on Smotinose Isle jany 14th 1813." The owner of Smuttynose Isle, Samuel Haley, had built a large square house on the island, with a broad balcony running the whole length of the house beneath the second-story windows. By tradition, he placed a lantern each night in his bedroom window, facing the southwest above the balcony facing the seacoast. That night when the *Sagunto* ran aground, "crashing full upon the fatal southeast point,…her costly timbers of mahoganyand cedar-wood were splintered on the sharp teeth of those inexorable rocks; her cargo of dried fruits and nuts and bales of broadcloth and gold and silver, was tossed about the shore, and part of her crew were thrown upon it."

The Spanish sailors struggled along the unfamiliar coastline. Two of them saw the light in Haley's window and made it as far as the stone seawall he'd built before the house. In the morning, Haley, his sons and others on the island discovered the destruction. As Thaxter wrote, "Fourteen bodies were found at that time, strewn all the way between the wall and that southeast point where the vessel had gone to pieces. The following summer the skeleton of another was discovered among some bushes near the shore."[112]

Long before the Colonial government began to maintain lighthouses along the coast, the responsibility for rescue rested on the citizens of the community, as did the installation of lighthouses and navigational aids for those ships passing by their shores. The first lighthouse constructed in New England was Boston Light on Little Brewster Island. In 1783, the Massachusetts legislature provided £1,400 to build a lighthouse on the site where a water tower had been damaged during the Revolutionary War. Workers constructed a seventy-five-foot conical stone tower that held several

Above: Postcard of Portland Head Light. *From the author's collection.*

Left: Old postcard of Minot's Light, near Boston, Massachusetts. *From the author's collection.*

lamps. Brant Point Light was built in Nantucket in 1746. Plymouth Light on Gurnet Point (1768) and Twin Lights on Thatcher Island (1771) followed in quick succession, though Plum Island did not get its lonely light until 1788.

Prominent citizens in the colony founded the Massachusetts Humane Society in 1785, which became the foundation of the American system of rescue from shipwreck. The organization established huts along the shore to provide shelter for stranded victims and built lifeboat stations manned by volunteers from the community. The Massachusetts lifeboat stations had grown to more than seventy by 1871, when Congress appropriated funds to create the United States Lifesaving Service.

A stone lighthouse was erected by the federal government at Portland Head in Maine and completed in January 1791. Four years later, a light was installed up the coast at Seguin Island, near the entrance to the Kennebec River. A quarter century later, another light was built on Pond Island, where troops had encamped during the War of 1812 to prevent the British from entering the river.

On Matinicus Rock, a barren outcrop of the island that lies past the entrance of Penobscot Bay, a lighthouse station was erected in 1827, with two wooden towers and a keeper's dwelling. The wooden towers were replaced by twin, stone towers about thirty years later, and "the Rock," as locals called it, would become the training ground for one of the first female keepers in the country.

In 1853, Samuel Burgess became keeper and moved his wife and four of their youngest children to the station. The eldest of these, fourteen-year-old Abigail, quickly learned the operation of the lamps and grew as proficient as her father in trimming the wicks and cleaning the reflective lenses of the beacons. Abbie, as she was called, came to be relied upon more and more as her mother was sickly and needed almost constant care and medicine. The Burgesses relied on supply boats that came on a quarterly schedule to the island and delivered the oil for the lamps, as well as provisions and the medicine Mrs. Burgess required.

In January 1856, however, the family found itself in dire straits. The supply boat had not come as it usually did in September, and while they had some food and oil to last awhile, the keeper knew they would run out before another boat arrived in the spring. Having little choice, Burgess set off for Rockland, twenty-five miles away, leaving Abbie in charge of the light and its keeping.

Almost immediately, a storm arrived offshore. Abbie dutifully maintained the twenty-five lamps that the towers held. As the cold grew worse, the thin strain of oil they had left to use for the lamps congealed quickly and had to be heated before being carried to the towers. The storm seemed not to abate. A week turned into two, and then by the nineteenth day of the month, the weather became worse, with high seas that threatened to engulf the tiny station. Abbie moved her family from the wooden keeper's cottage into one of the new towers, hoping it would prove stable enough to protect them. As she later wrote of the ordeal, "As the tide came, the sea rose higher and higher, till the only endurable places were the lighttowers. If they stood, we were saved, otherwise our fate was only too certain."

It was a fortuitous move, for just hours later, the family watched from the safety of the tower as the furious sea breached the Rock and swept the cottage away.

Even as sleet and snow pounded the lights, Abbie worked hard to keep the beacons shining, clearing the lenses of ice and hoarfrost daily until the storm finally subsided. The seas continued to be rough, and it was nearly a month before her father was able to return.

When a new keeper was installed at the lights four years later, it was Abbie who stayed and trained him, as well as his son Isaac to assist with the duties required. They worked together for several months, and it was no surprise to anyone who knew them that Abigail and Isaac were married within that year. The couple continued to live on the Rock, with Isaac eventually appointed keeper and Abbie receiving the salary of a keeper's assistant. Together, they raised four children on the tiny island. Abbie was also promoted to keeper in 1872 and assigned to White Head Light. She and her husband continued in the lifesaving service until retirement in 1890.

The story of the courageous actions of her youth became a popular children's story and later a musical. As for Abigail, she told her story in letters. As she wrote late in her life, she often dreamed about "those old lights on Maniticus Rock...When I dream of them it always seems to me that I have been away from them for a long while, and I am hurrying toward the Rock to light the lamps before sunset."

Hendrick's Head Light, on the east side of the entrance to the Sheepscot River, would also become the scene of a long-told legend. In March 1870, keeper Jarial Marr and his wife witnessed a wreck offshore and could clearly see that those on board had climbed into the rigging, where they were desperately clinging and in real danger of being frozen to death. The sea was too rough to launch a dory, so the couple were forced to wait for the waters to calm and to watch the stricken ship. Toward dusk, Marr noticed a bundle floating to shore. He pulled it from the waves with

Lighthouse Station at Matinicus Rock, circa 1890. *From* America's Lighthouses, An Illustrated History.

Postcard of New Haven Lighthouse. *From the author's collection.*

a boathook and saw that it was two featherbed mattresses roped together with a box between them. When the keeper opened the box, he found a baby girl inside. The keeper's descendants still tell the tale today and claim that the little girl, named Seaborn, was adopted by a wealthy couple who were summer residents.

The Marr family was to provide three generations of keepers and lifesaving volunteers. When Wolcott Marr rescued the crew of a wrecked schooner in 1914, he had his sons beside him in the lifeboat.

Connecticut erected its first light at New London harbor in 1761. A sixty-four-foot wooden tower, it escaped the fate of many short-lived wooden lighthouses and was ceded to the federal government in 1790, replaced by a octagonal brownstone tower in 1801. A thirty-five-foot wooden tower was erected at Lynde Point in 1802, and in 1805, a similar tower was constructed at Five Mile Point—the distance from the light to New Haven. In 1831, a light station was established at Morgan Point to aid in navigation at the entrance to the Mystic River. The following year, a single stone tower with a separate stone dwelling was built at the east entrance of Stonington Harbor.

In Rhode Island, early settlers erected a watch house at Beavertail Point as early as 1705. By 1712, a lighted beacon was used, tended to in part by local Narragansett Indians. The first lighthouse on the point was constructed in 1749 and was a sixty-nine-foot wooden tower. This burned a few years later, and another was erected by 1753; this survived until the British burned the tower in October 1779.

Narragansett settlers had erected a wooden beacon on Point Judith during colonial times. A more permanent structure was built in 1810 but destroyed in the Great Gale of 1815. The light was then replaced by a stone tower[113] that rose to a height of seventy-five feet and was fitted with ten whale lamps fixed to a revolving table to provide a flashing light. The power was supplied by a 288-pound weight that dropped through a channel in the tower, taking approximately 144 seconds to perform a complete revolution.[114]

There was initially no keeper's cottage, but a farmhouse some three hundred yards north of the tower served this purpose until 1857 when the Point Judith Lighthouse was rebuilt as it presently stands, with the bottom half of the tower painted white and the upper half brown, with an attached dwelling that housed the keeper's family and assistant. In 1872, a station and boathouse for the U.S. Life Saving Service was erected on the lighthouse grounds, and by 1890, the installation of mantles and the use of kerosene oil greatly intensified the beacon. In 1903, a telegraph station was installed outside the lighthouse, and this greatly reduced the number of ships in peril, as conditions and locations could be sent by cable to ships still far off the dangerous reefs. The oil-lit beacons remained in use until 1935, when electricity was installed in the tower.

On Block Island, the first lighthouse constructed was North Light in 1829. A stone, double-lighted tower, it was quickly eroded by the elements and replaced several times before a retaining wall was built, and a large stone building, with a light attached, was constructed in 1868. The massive granite blocks for the building are said to have been sent from quarries by schooner to the island and then hauled in oxcarts from the beach to Sandy Point.

Lighthouse engraved on a tombstone in Plymouth, Massachusetts. *Courtesy of the author.*

The Southeast Light was constructed in 1875 with much fanfare. The Italianate and Gothic brick building with a stone foundation was an architectural showcase for Block Island in its heyday as a haven for wealthy summer residents. The lighthouse quickly became one of the most photographed buildings on the island and was far enough away from Old Harbor and the hotels to be a fair bicycling excursion.

Keepers of the lighthouse remained in the Clark family for a span of forty years, and a descendant on the island recalled that her grandfather "could smell fog before anyone could see it, and he'd always have the boilers going for the fog signal before it was needed."

Postcard of Goat Island Light. *From the author's collection.*

Newport, which had been occupied during the war, had its first light constructed on the northern tip of Goat Island at the entrance to the harbor. The original twenty-foot tower was replaced by a thirty-five-foot tower in 1842. With the increase of maritime traffic in the harbor, the Lime Rock Light was constructed on the ledges some nine hundred feet offshore.

Hosea Lewis was appointed the light's first keeper, but it was his daughter Idawalley, better known as Ida, who would receive national attention for her unfailing efforts to rescue those in peril at sea. Lewis had been a cutter pilot and was familiar with rescues at sea. He taught his daughter the techniques needed to keep a rowboat steady in a gale and how to draw victims over the stern so as to not capsize the boat. These skills would fall to Ida when the keeper fell ill a few years after his tenure began.

Her first rescue was in the fall of 1858, at age sixteen, when she rescued four boys clinging to their capsized sailboat. The boys, from well-to-do families, had set out in a small catboat for a picnic on "the dumplings," a rocky island that had been the site of a fort during the Revolutionary War. They reached the island and had their repast but, on the return, found it difficult to tack in the northwesterly wind and so slackened the sail and counted on the tide to take them onto Jones Beach.

They soon grew restless, and one boy shimmied up the mast to see how far off they were from shore. The movement and weight caused the boat to sway, and the subsequent panicked motions of the boys capsized the craft.

Ida had witnessed the entire scene and was rowing swiftly toward them as they cried for help and tried to cling to the hull. One by one, she pulled the waterlogged boys into the rowboat, and the last, Samuel Powell, fell unconscious as they were rowed to the light. The shivering would-be sailors were given blankets and hot toddies. Young Powell was revived with the aid of stimulants. Although Ida had demonstrated great courage and skill in rescuing the boys, it was hardly noticed in the community of "summer people." The boys were too ashamed to tell their parents what had happened, and only Samuel Powell among them reportedly thanked the young keeper for saving him. It was not until eleven years—and scores of rescues—later when *Harper's Weekly* magazine ran an article on the lighthouse heroine, and others soon followed suit.

In May 1869, the Rhode Island General Assembly passed a petition, which read in part, "This General Assembly desires to recognize officially the heroism of Miss Ida Lewis, of Newport, in repeatedly saving the lives of drowning men, at the risk of her own and we are proud that one of our own citizens, by her courage and humanity, has won admiration of the whole country."

Despite these adulations, Ida was not officially appointed keeper of Lime Rock Light until 1879, nearly two years after a rescue that involved three soldiers who had capsized in a storm and whom Ida rowed back safely through sleet and snow to the station. Her brother Rud remarked to the newspapers, "Ida knows how to handle a boat. She can hold one to wind'ard in a gale better than any man I ever saw wet an oar, and yes, do it too, when the sea is breaking over her."

Governor Ambrose Burnside promoted the appointment of Ida Lewis as keeper and ushered it through the Lighthouse Board as one of his final acts as chief executive. It is estimated that during her tenure as keeper of Lime Rock Light, Ida was responsible for the rescue of as many as thirty-five people. Included among them were three men and the valuable sheep they had been transporting for banker August Belmont. In its heyday as a fashionable resort for Victorian vacationers, a visit to Lime Rock and the famous keeper became a popular pastime for those in the area. Visitors flooded the harbor in all manner of craft to visit the "female Hercules."

In 1881, Ida was awarded a gold Life Saving Medal of First Class by an act of Congress. She was the first woman to receive such an honor. Ida Lewis continued in the Life Saving Service and performed her last rescue at the age of sixty-four. She tended the light to her last, when on October 21, 1911, she suffered a massive stroke after extinguishing the flame of the lamp that morning.

In death, Ida was remembered for her heroism. Her large granite gravestone adorned with oars and a solemn tribute attests to the respect she acquired for her courageous efforts over the years. After her death, many speculated that the Lime Rock Lighthouse would be decommissioned, and

in fact, it was under consideration by the Lighthouse Board. A groundswell of historical sentiment for the structure that many locals had called "Ida Lewis Light" since they could remember gained over the coming years, spurred on by U.S. Representative Clark Burdick, who in 1924 succeeded in having the station named after the keeper.

When it was officially decommissioned three years later, a new challenge arose to save the light and the island. Dr. Horace Beck, a prominent resident of Newport, was resolved to save the historic light and made inquiries with the government, which had installed an automated light on a steel tower on the island but let the keeper's cottage fall into disrepair. The doctor enlisted the help of his friend and philanthropist Arthur Curtiss James, and the two formed the Narragansett Bay Regatta Association and purchased the lighthouse and much of the island. With their efforts, and those of others, the Ida Lewis Yacht Club opened its doors in the renovated cottage on July 24, 1924.

The keeper's name is now associated with several organizations around the community, and Ida remains a role model for young woman even into the twenty-first century.

The busy west passage of Narragansett Bay determined that a light be built at Warwick Neck in 1826, and on the east side of the entrance to the Providence River, a light was constructed at Nyatt Point two years later in the form of an octagonal brick tower and a separate dwelling. These were badly damaged in a gale in 1855, and a new twenty-five-foot square tower was constructed the following year.

By the mid-nineteenth century, there were nine lifesaving stations along the coast of Rhode Island. There are many stories of the heroic efforts of the men and women who manned these stations, but the following example exacts perhaps a more typical narrative of what the crew of these stations endured in their day-to-day duties. Captain Herbert Knowles, of the Point Judith, Rhode Island Lifesaving Station, was asked by historian Horace Belcher to recall a rescue from forty-seven years before, and the captain replied in writing, "I will endeavor to answer your inquiries relative to the collision of the schooners…I do not remember very much of the details now having been to so many disasters."

Opposite, top: *Harper's Weekly* illustration of a storm at Lime Rock Light (1869).

Opposite, bottom: Grave of Ida Lewis in the cemetery off Farewell Street in Newport, Rhode Island.

Point Judith Lifesaving Station. *From the author's collection.*

Crew of the Point Judith Lighthouse and Lifesaving Station (1877). *Courtesy of Henry A.L. Brown.*

Nonetheless, Captain Knowles's account of his memories of the events following the night of December 25, 1885, when the *Willie De Wolf,* westward bound and laden with timber, and the *Mott Haven,* headed east and carrying a mixed cargo of goods and coal, collided off the coast of Rhode Island. Captain Knowles and his crew learned of the disaster at breakfast the next morning:

We lost no time in getting the rest of the crew up and clothed with oil skins and launching the boat. The cook in the mean time [sic] *dunked the biscuts, fried beef and grease into a cedar pail and put it in the boat. No one had eaten a mouthful. It was rough and no easy task to get clear of the shore and rocks without staving the boat. The* De Wolf *was reached about a quarter of nine. On finding no one[,] we kept down to the* Mott Haven *knowing the crew, if any, would be sheltered in the vessel[']s topsails. Finding no one[,] we made a strange effort to pull back. The boys were all stout and experienced* [but] *could make no headway[,] so I decided to run for Block Island while the men were fairly fresh. The wind was behind us, and fast increasing, as was also the sea. For the first four and a half miles or more[,] we ran through all kinds of debris—laths, timber etc from the* Willie De Wolf *and chairs, tables, stools, sofas, and all kinds of barrels from the cargo of the* Mott Haven. *When in the belly of the seas[,] we didn't seem to get very little wind and the boat could take a few strokes with the oars but had to lift them as the stern of the boat raised on the sea following. By the time I felt the wind on back of my head[,] the boat would start to run on the sea like a sled sliding down a steep hill for nearly ⅛ of a mile turning a high wave from the bluff of each bow and vibrating every part of her from stern to stern. It would have been fatal for an oar to have come in contact with the water when the boat was running on the sea…I steered the boat with both oar and rudder, the latter by pressing my hip against the tiller. It was no easy matter to handle her and keep her from broaching to which of course would have ended it. The compass was of little use more than to glance at occasionally and judge the course by general average. Due allowance was made for the tide[,] which proved to help make the course perfect. For when the Island was first sighted through the rifts* [of] *sea smoke[,] the old harbor was straight ahead. The basin being full of boats and schooners[,] I decided to land on the beach west of it. It seemed as if tho the whole population of the Island came down to greet us.*[115]

Woman waiting for her sailor's return. *Illustration from Whittier's* Ballads of New England.

As it happened, the crew of the *Mott Haven* had taken the ship's yawl and made for Block Island, reaching the shore about five o'clock in the morning, and were by then in the care of the New Shoreham Lifesaving Station. The captain and crew members of the *De Wolf* had been picked up by a passing vessel and taken into Newport. In that age of poor communication, relying on signals and lights, which were rarely seen during a storm, each community responded on word of a wreck and, without hesitation, placed the lives of their keepers and volunteers in harm's way to affect a rescue.

As compelling as these narratives and written memoirs may be, the true story of the relationship New Englanders had with their loved ones while at sea can only be recounted in the letters to those men at sea and those written by sailors to their wives or sweethearts at home. In addition, there were many journals kept by men and women during this period, as well as "observations" and poems written in weathered remark books of the era.

Historian Elizabeth Shure, in her essay "Whaling Letters," wrote that women left behind during the typical three years of a whaling cruise "had to endure these long separations, the care of family, the household, and property, as well and the constant bitter fear of disaster 'somewhere.'"

In 1802, thirty-seven-year-old Phebe Folger Coleman, of Nantucket, wrote to her husband, Captain Samuel Coleman, "I have felt a little guilty that I have deferred so long to write: but I had nothing worth communicating,

Illustration from Whittier's Ballads of New England.

nothing but what thou might reasonably suppose, that is, I am very lonesome. Why should so much of our time be spent apart? Why do we refuse the happiness within our reach?"[116]

In May 1837, another Nantucket woman wrote of her neighbor's hardship: "Elisa had a letter from Shibael about a week ago…he was well, and we are very thankful to hear that. The time had begun to seem very long since she had heard it was 16 months that there had been no correct news he has been absent from home 3 years the 25th day of this month and she does not look for him before next November if he should live."[117]

Among the historians who have given us insight into the lives of these women, Lisa Norling has shown that the wives of New Bedford proved to be proficient in maintaining home and property, even maintaining a network of support among other wives and relatives in seaside communities. She wrote, "Women in New Bedford or other urban centers earned money by accepting various kinds of piecework, especially sewing, or taking in borders, or purveying many different kinds of goods in small shops."

The same was true in Nantucket, where one of the main thoroughfares was known as "Petticoat Row" for some time while its shops were run by the wives and widows of the whale men. But as the considerable research conducted by Ruth Wallis Herndon has revealed, women in other communities faced extreme hardship while their husbands were at sea.

Postcard of North Light and Sandy Point, Block Island. *From the author's collection.*

In the absence of what the colony deemed a head of household, town councilmen took up the cases of dependent women and children, often splitting up families by "warning out" families of sailors who had fallen destitute, an act that ultimately permitted the council to move the family from its jurisdiction to the place of the absent husband's birth. In many instances, this moved whole families inland from the seaside communities and their network of support for wives of seamen. As Herndon shows, however, if the family was "in a poor, low & deplorable state and condition," a sailor's wife had little choice but to plead for assistance.

This is what Sarah Tripp of Tiverton faced with her husband gone for two years, a good twelve months before the "three years' absence" the law generally required to declare a man lost at sea. She petitioned the town and received permission to sell land in order to support herself and her children.

In many cases, however, the town counsel saw fit to bind out children in apprenticeships to local tradesmen in order to cut the cost of the dependents to the town. Children suffered these and other hardships while their fathers and uncles were at sea. In many cases, the children grew up largely in their fathers' absences, and despite pleas in letters to "remember me to them," a Nantucket woman wrote of the experience many children shared:

> *One day two children had been playing together on Steamboat Wharf in a sail loft which belonged to the father of one of these little maidens. The*

112

boat from New Bedford had "blown" and was docking. "Come, Lizzie, quick, quick!" One of the girls was hurried by her uncle to a group of sea captains, all known to her except the one in the center, whom they were welcoming. "Well, Lizzie Plaskett, who's this?" was the question. "I don't know," she answered, quite abashed by the stranger's eyes, "unless it's my cousin George Henry Brock, home from sea." "No, child, no!" cried the man, catching her up in his arms. "It's your own father. Run and tell mother that I've come to surprise her."[118]

This experience was popularized in verse by Charles Clauson in the poem "Nursery Ryme of Innocence and Experience," the opening stanzas of which have a young boy meeting a sea captain and making a request:

I had a silver penny
And an apricot tree
And I said to the sailor
On the white quay
Sailor O' Sailor
Will you bring me
If I give you my penny
And my apricot tree
A fez from Algeria
An Arab drum to beat
A little gilt sword
And a parakeet?

The sailor promises to bring the boy "presents back from the sea." Three years later, the boy is met on the same wharf by a different sailor with the presents from the mariner he befriended, but this baffles the now-older boy:

O where is the sailor
With bold red hair?
And what is that volley
On the bright air?
O where are the other
Girls and boys?
And why have you brought me
Children's toys?

A captain or sailor might place his fate on the mercy of the sea in order to earn a decent living, but he by no means left thoughts of home and loved ones behind. The wealth of seaman's journals and letters attest to a love of home and family within their pages.

Captain Charles E. Alien, writing to his daughter while aboard the bark *Sea Ranger*, noted despondently:

> *Dear daughter Emma, as I have been sitting here in my cabin, alone and lonely, the thought rushed into my mind: Is this all of life? My heart answered No...I must, if spared return to my home at Nantucket, Four years farther on toward the end of my Pilgrimage, worn down in body, unfit for labor at home, and temporally poorer than when I embarked: but I have a hope that all this is not to be and that the End will produce a brighter and newer beautiful picture...Yet we may be spared to again meet those from whom we are now far separated.*[119]

In late February 1863, after a week of rough weather, Captain John R. Congdon of East Greenwich, Rhode Island, wrote in his diary aboard the *Caroline Tucker*, "I am tired of Cape Horn. Hope and pray we shall get clearly around by, if so catch me never again. I have made an oath if I get home all right, before I come again I hope to be blind so I can't see so as to be able to come to sea. I have promised never to give her another voyage."[120]

Congdon's wife, Cynthia, had accompanied her husband on his whaling journeys from 1852 through 1859. She had been aboard all but his last two voyages, but now she waited for his return once more at their home on Greenwich Bay. Captain Congdon's passage aboard the *Caroline Tucker* would be his last. A letter from the ship's owner informed his son that the misfortune he and his mother both feared had occurred in Cape Horn's treacherous waters. Congdon had been washed overboard "in a heavy gale of wind...Every effort was made to save Capt. Congdon without avail... That those he has left behind may be reunited to him in that better land where gales and tempests are unknown is the wish of your friend."[121]

From America, there came an increasingly religious population of sailors among the rovers; hence the written sentiment of Silvanus Crosby at the beginning of his remark book:

> *Nantucket is my dwelling place and*
> *Christ is my salvation.*
> *When I am dead and in my grave*
> *And all my bones are rotten*

Postcard of the Seaman's Bethel in New Bedford. *From the author's collection.*

This you see remember me and
Don't let me be forgotten.

Crosby needn't have worried. He would come to serve as a captain and live to be seventy-one and buried in the Old North Cemetery of "his dwelling place." For those sailors who did not have families or who faced long years apart from their wives and children, seaman's bethels played an increasingly important role as havens for body and soul. The most famous of these would become the Seaman's Bethel built in New Bedford, Massachusetts.

Constructed by the New Bedford Port Society in 1832, the bethel became famous after its inclusion in the American classic *Moby Dick*, in which Melville wrote of the whaling town where "there stands a Whaleman's Chapel, and few are the moody fishermen, shortly bound for the Indian Ocean or Pacific, who fail to make a Sunday visit to the spot."

Conceived in the 1820s, the bethel grew out of increasing concern by those same Christians leading temperance and anti-gambling movements about the "arduous and licentious lifestyles of the nearly 5,000 seamen employed at this port." The port society was soon incorporated with a dedication to "the moral and religious improvement of seamen," and the mariners' chapel began to be constructed. The American Seaman's Friends Society began in 1828 and soon set up bethel churches in many ports frequented by British and American sailors.

In their efforts to convert and to keep steady the "rudder of their faithful path," societies gave out Bibles and printed religious pamphlets to remind sailors of their salvation. One such pamphlet printed in New York was distributed along the eastern seaboard, titled, "The Shipwreck: Showing What Sometimes Happens on the Seacoasts also Giving a Particular Account of 'A Poor Sailor Boy', Who Was Refused Any Assistance by the Wreckers, and Who Died in Consequence of Their Inhuman Conduct." It was printed by the American Tract Society and distributed to sailors from New York to Nantucket. The long poem begins with every sailor's deep dread:

In Winter's rude storm, when the tempests blow loud,
and the hail drives full hard 'gainst the door,...

'Tis then the poor Bark often sinks in the wave,
and brave seamen go down to the dead;

ERECTED
By the Officers and crew of the
Bark A.R.Tucker of New Bedford
To the memory of
CHARLES H. PETTY,
of Westport, Mass.
who died Dec. 14$\frac{t}{7}$ 1863,
in the 18$\frac{th}{7}$ year of his age.
His death occured in nine hours
after being bitten by a shark,
while bathing near the ship,
He was buried by his shipmates
on the Island of DeLoss, near
the Coast of Africa.

Cenotaph in the interior of
the Seaman's Bethel, New
Bedford, Massachusetts.
Courtesy of the author.

no harbor, no vessel, nor mortal to save,
to snatch one poor soul from a watery grave,
or in pity to hold up his head.

The "poor sailor boy" of the narrative does indeed survive a shipwreck,
only to lay dying with others on the shore where "the rock's craggy cliff was
their last lonely bed," while the "wreckers," or wicked townsfolk, gather the
goods coming to shore and ignore the pleas of the dying seamen. The village
vicar comes and attends to the dying and comforts the boy:

What though yonder wreckers live out a long day,
and thyself find an early, rough grave;
though the wicked appear to succeed in their way,
and the kind-hearted seaman becomes their fell prey,
yet the righteous forever he'll save.

Not save from all troubles of life's stormy day,
but from evil's hereafter to come;
oft as death finds their feet treading duty's safe way,
still aiming their Savior to love and obey,
He conveys their blest spirits straight home.[122]

The bethels were also places of remembrance. In New Bedford's chapel alone, there are thirty-one black-framed cenotaphs that bear the names of whale men and fishermen who were lost at sea. Twenty-three cenotaphs predate 1900. Most of the early cenotaphs memorialize individuals who were lost overboard during whaling voyages and give an account of the tragedy. More recent tablets list the names, dates and vessels of New Bedford–area fishermen lost at sea. Some cenotaphs pay tribute to entire crews who were lost with their vessels.[123]

CHAPTER 7

Stories from the Stones

For those lost at sea, their names and circumstances of death might be inscribed on the pages of a ship's log, in the port registry, in poetry or even on the walls of a seaman's chapel, but the most enduring testimony or memorials would be those inscribed in stone, though it might be years before a lost sailor had a memorial at home or shared one with a relative who died later.

An example of this is the simple tombstone in Providence's North Burial Ground erected by the mother of young Thomas Cranston, who died at the untimely age of twenty-nine. Inscribed below his name and dates of birth and death is a memorial line to his father, who was "lost at sea March 1799, in his 26th year."

A similar story is engraved on a stone in Newport, Rhode Island. It reads:

> *Abigail relict of Henry Castoff and of her son*
> *Captain Charles Castoff who died onboard the Brig Poland on*
> *His passage from Havana to Savannah, Aug. 23, 1842 Aged 26 years.*

Throughout the seaside communities of southern New England, one finds stories of the fate of so many seamen. In Newport's Old Cemetery, we find a few examples of these, including those memorials above an empty grave:

Above: Grave of Thomas Cranston, North Burial Ground, Providence, Rhode Island. *Courtesy of the author.*

Left: Gravestone of mother and her son who was buried at sea. North Burial Ground, Providence, Rhode Island. *Courtesy of the author.*

Grave of Henry Tew in the old cemetary off Farewell Street, Newport, Rhode Island. *Courtesy of the author.*

Capt. Elisha C. Rodman departed this life Nov. 11, 1802
In the 27th year of his age on the coast of Africa and was buried
on the Island Of St. Thomas

A similar fate befell Captain Henry Tew, who died in the same waters fifteen years later but was likely buried at sea.

Memorials for military veterans often take a place of prominence among the simpler stones in any nineteenth-century cemetery park, and the North Burial Ground holds several examples of these. One such memorial is the solid block of granite dedicated to the memory of Captain John R. Dennis, "lost on Long Island Sound" on February 3, 1849. The stone was likely erected on the death of his wife, Hope Ann Rhodes, in 1862, but just four years later, an inscription for their son, Frank Dennis, a first lieutenant in the Eleventh Rhode Island volunteers, was added when he was "lost aboard the S.S. *Evening Star*" in October 1866.

Grave of First Lieutenant Frank Dennis, lost at sea in 1866. North Burial Ground, Providence, Rhode Island. *Courtesy of the author.*

Another naval memorial dating from the Civil War is the limestone crypt of Ensign Francis Gardner Adams, whose remarkable record of service was written in Joseph Russell Bartlett's *Memoirs of Rhode Island Officers*, published in 1867.

Adams enlisted in the navy at the end of August 1861 and began to study gunnery and small arms at the Washington Naval Yard. He was soon ordered on the steamship frigate *Susquehanna*. Captain's mate Adams joined the vessel only two days after its return from a bruising engagement that had killed about forty sailors among the American fleet of seventy-nine vessels. The fleet had left port with eighty-four ships but had lost five in a gale on their way to the engagement.

Despite this ominous beginning, Adams was soon engaged in the routine activities aboard the ship as it patrolled the coast of Florida. He also saw his first action as the ship was part of the capture of Fort Clinch and Fernandina. It was also among the detail assigned to attack the ironclad vessel the *Merrimack*.

On May 28, 1862, the *Susquehannah* sailed for the Gulf of Mexico to join the squadron of Admiral Farragut, enforcing the blockade of Mobile, Alabama. The ship served with the squadron for nearly a year before returning to New York in May 1863. Once there, Adams was assigned to the ship *Savannah*, on which he was promoted to the rank of ensign. On the August 10, he joined the gunboat *Aires*, which was soon part of the patrol of Charleston Harbor. Adams was next ordered aboard the ironclad *Weehawken*, which, "during the few days he was attached to this vessel…was constantly engaged with the rebel batteries."[124]

He was next ordered to join the crew of the captured *Atlanta* and served aboard the ship as it was taken to Philadelphia. Adams briefly fell ill while in the city but on recovery was assigned to the gunboat *Chenango* and was on board during the explosion of the boiler while the ship sat in New York Harbor, which killed twenty-eight of his shipmates. Ensign Adams was ordered to the ironclad monitor *Manhattan* on April 21, 1864, but by May was aboard the supply steamship *Union*, and then in September, he was ordered aboard his old ship, the *Susquehanna*.

By October 1864, he was again aboard the *Union* on passage to Key West, where he was ordered to the gunboat *Honduras*. The vessel was deployed in early May, but Adams fell ill with dysentery aboard ship, and on its return on May 13, he was taken ashore. There he flirted with recovery, first in the naval hospital and then in a private residence, where he suffered a relapse and died on May 22, 1865.

Another memorial was erected in Newport years later for a naval seaman: "Robert Ingham lost on the U.S. Sloop of War Huron Nov. 21, 1877 aged 49 years…served his country well for 21 years and 7 months." And in the same cemetery, we find another for a sailor whose service had barely begun. Eighteen-year-old Horatio R. Brown was "lost from U.S.S. Kearsarge, at Fortress Munroe May 1, 1881."

A prevalent disaster could also compel a family to raise a memorable monument, such as the striking, though now damaged, memorial to Captain Thomas Green Hull, who was found a little more than a week after leaving New York for Baltimore on December 21, 1864, "lashed to the mast of his sunken and ill fated vessel." The thirty-two-year-old Hull's grandfather had been a mariner, and his father, Thomas Hull, was one of the most influential

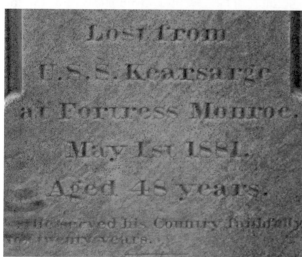

Above: Crypt of Francis Gardner Adams, North Burial Ground, Providence, Rhode Island. *Courtesy of the author.*

Left: Inscription from the grave of Robert Ingham, Old Burial Ground, Newport, Rhode Island. *Courtesy of the author*

CAPT.
THOMAS GREEN HULL
BORN AUG. 7, 1832,
LEFT NEW YORK FOR BALTIMORE
DEC. 21, 1864
AND ON DEC. 30, 1864, WAS FOUND
LASHED TO THE MAST OF HIS
SUNKEN AND ILL-FATED VESSEL.
AGED 32 YEARS, 4 MONTHS
AND 4 DAYS.

Oh! blessed are they who die like him,
loved with such love,
And with such sorrow mourned.

The long-damaged monument to Thomas Green Hull, North Burial Ground, Providence, Rhode Island. *Courtesy of the author.*

captains and packet owners in Providence. A descendant of Hull confirmed that the story had come down in the family for generations, tradition being that he lashed himself to the mast when he knew all was lost so that the family might find his body.[125]

As might be expected, longevity often brought greater renown in the community, and thus, the memorial for that "Notable Mystic Sea Captain" Albert Crary Burrows, whose community etched his biography in stone:

> *His marine career began at age 14 when he shipped out as "boy" on the whale ship "Romulus." This trip lasted for more than three years and circled the entire globe.*
>
> *Captain Burrows crossed the Atlantic Ocean over 100 times. On many of these trips he commanded ships of the famous Mallory Line. He was first married to Betsey Haley and later to Nellie Shanahan.*
>
> *Lost at sea 1904*

The ordinary seamen and fishermen, if receiving memorials at all, were given smaller stones and simpler descriptions denoting their stature, as we saw with the description of the Cranston memorial stone earlier. On occasion, a friend's good humor could make their resting place memorable to the living, such as the epitaph for the captain of a fishing boat lost at sea that many curious tourists notice in a cemetery on Block Island:

> *Captain Thomas Coffin*
> *Died 1842 aged 50 years*
> *He's done a-catching cod*
> *And gone to meet his God*

Today, these lines—both solemn and irreverent—inscribed on stone remain testament to the family's loss and their remembrance of those long-written wishes from their sailors that they not be forgotten. They are also often the first step for local historians in unfolding their stories from the end to their beginning and then full circle to their end once more.

A Ship Lost, Another Reborn

The age of sail is now long past memory, revisited in modern times by the more than seventy-six tall ships that sail individually and "in company" at festivals around the world. As anyone who has witnessed a parade of tall ships can attest, it is a magnificent sight.

But tourist festivals bring only the barest semblance of what a seaman living during the age of sail faced each day. For that experience, or the closest that it may be replicated in our high-tech times, was to serve aboard one of these ships, like the HMS *Bounty*.

The three-masted, 180-foot vessel was originally built for the 1962 film *Mutiny on the* Bounty. After the movie was completed, the ship was docked in Florida for some years before being purchased, along with the movie rights, by Ted Turner in 1986.

The communications mogul offered to donate the vessel to a community that would maintain the ship, and the city of Fall River, Massachusetts, submitted the winning proposal to take ownership. Under the guardianship of the Tall Ship Bounty Foundation, the vessel served many years on the Fall River waterfront, a highlight being when it joined a parade of sail in Boston in 1997. By 2001, however, the foundation could no longer maintain the vessel, and the *Bounty* was sold to Long Island businessman Robert E. Hansen, who had the ship fully restored in Boothbay Harbor, Maine, as well as coast guard certified to sail again. Its home port became Greenport, New York, but the *Bounty* spent its summers sailing the eastern seaboard as an active participant of Tall Ships America.

In late October 2012, with Hurricane Sandy approaching the East Coast of the United States from across the Atlantic, it was advised that the ship sail for calmer waters to ride out the storm. This was not unprecedented. During its stay in Fall River, the Coast Guard had advised the vessel to head out to sea and ride out the devastating Hurricane Andrew in 1992.

On Friday, October 26, the *Bounty*, under command of its sixty-three-year-old veteran captain Robin Walbridge, departed New London with a crew of sixteen, bound for St. Petersburg, Florida. The vessel's tall ships website posted promising news on Saturday, October 27, writing, "It now looks like the ship…has successfully slipped past the path of the storm and is sailing south and west as the hurricane tracks north toward the northeast coast. The captain estimates that the ship and the hurricane will pass each other on opposite courses sometime Sunday night or Monday morning."

A posting from Captain Walbridge on Sunday, however, seemed to voice concern. He wrote, "I think we're going to be into this for several days…we are just going to keep trying to go fast and squeeze by the storm and land as fast as we can."

Sometime that Sunday evening, the ship began taking on water. When the pumps failed and the vessel began to founder, the crew took to two lifeboats and abandoned ship about ninety miles southeast of Cape Hatteras, North Carolina. Captain Walbridge stayed with the ship.

The coast guard rescued fourteen crew by helicopter, but missing were forty-two-year-old crew member Claudene Christian and Captain Walbridge, though the masts of the sunken ship were still visible above the eighteen-foot swells. The body of Ms. Christian was recovered Monday evening. The search for Captain Robin Walbridge was conducted for several weeks. He is presumed lost at sea.

In the wake of that tragedy, another ship was being reborn. The *Charles W. Morgan* was built as a whaling vessel at the Hillman Brothers Shipyard in New Bedford in 1841, and between its launching and retirement in 1921, it completed thirty-seven voyages, surviving the perils of numerous storms, arctic ice flows and even an attack from South Pacific islanders. It's little wonder that it became known as a lucky ship.

After its retirement, it was purchased by E.H.R. Green, the son of one of its many captains over the years, and he kept the boat moored in the sandy cove off his estate in New Bedford. The ship was featured in three silent films, but Green died before making any definitive plans for the ship's future preservation. In 1941, the Maritime Historical Society of Stonington, Connecticut, stepped in and purchased the deteriorating whaler. The society hoped that the *Morgan* would become a much-needed feature attraction for its museum. Within months, the museum was receiving calls from other period boat owners, and a groundswell of support in the seaside community grew and finally culminated in the christening of the Mystic Seaport Museum in 1948. The ship became much more than a famous attraction, as acknowledged by current museum president Stephen C. White. The ship became an integral part of education and fundraising that has paid off handsomely for the museum's many projects. Restoration on the ship had been done in 1968 and again in 1974. Restorers estimate that after those repairs, only 30 percent of the original ship remained intact. The Mystic Seaport Foundation began to raise money for a most ambitious undertaking to restore the ship to its original form and put it out to sea as a floating, educational extension of the museum. The foundation eventually raised the $7 million needed for the project.

This latest and most extensive restoration began in 2008, with the ship landlocked and supported by metal braces, and then wrapped in plastic to protect it from the elements as crews inspected the vessel. They found that the futtocks, or "ribs," of the ship were rotted, and large parts of the bow and stern had also deteriorated beyond repair.

The restoration team, led by Quentin Snedicker, the head of the Seaport's Henry B. DuPont Preservation Shipyard, set out to re-create those parts needed. As a National Historical Landmark, an honor bestowed on the ship in 1966, period tools had to be used to create each rib, plank and trunnel by hand. Materials also had to be from the period: white pine planking replaced the original hull, black locust was used for the trunnels and live oak was found for the deck supports. White oak was used for the bow and stern. For some materials, the restorers recovered blow downs from the southern states after hurricanes had ripped through the region.

The thick replacement planking had to be steamed for three hours before the wood became flexible enough to bend and fit the curved places of the hull. Workers had to quickly nail the planking with brass spikes and wooden pegs before the planks dried out and split or cracked.

For Snedicker, the restoration not only brought the ship back to the life of a working vessel, but it also gave his crew a learning experience on how a wooden ship of the era was built, and those restorers, in turn, will pass the skills along to younger hands. As sail maker Nathaniel Wilson told the *Providence Journal*, "No one alive can remember the *Morgan* sailing. With this, you just don't restore the memory of the ship, you restore the living memory of it sailing. For me, that has far more value."

On June 23, 2013, the *Charles W. Morgan* was let loose from its cradle and slipped into the Mystic River. It will lie at the wharf for another year while new masts, spars and rigging are constructed. The ship will leave its berth in the spring of 2014 and be on the open water for the first time in ninety-three years. Its first non-whaling voyage is expected to take the ship to the ports of Newport, New London, New Bedford, Boston and the Massachusetts Maritime Academy for the centennial of the Cape Cod Canal. The *Morgan* will no longer fill its hold with whale oil and bone but be full of knowledge and information for the visitors who climb aboard the last wooden whale ship in the world.

Notes

Introduction

1. Carrol, "Journal."
2. Barlow, *Journal: Life At Sea.*
3. Rediker, *Between the Devil*, 156.

Chapter 1

4. Linebaugh and Rediker, *The Many-Headed Hydra*, 150.
5. Ibid.
6. Ibid., 151.
7. Rediker, *Between the Devil*, 295.
8. Morison, *Maritime History of Massachusetts*, 11.
9. Ibid.
10. Gillis, *The Human Shore*, 96.
11. Ibid., 97.
12. Ibid., 18.
13. Johnston, *The Yankee Fleet*, 36.
14. Hitchings, "Guarding the New England Coast," from *Seafaring in Colonial Massachusetts.*
15. Kurtz, *Bluejackets in the Blubber Room*, 4.

16. Gillis, *The Human Shore*, 110.
17. Hitchings, "Guarding the New England Coast," from *Seafaring in Colonial Massachusetts.*
18. Morison, *Maritime History of Massachusetts.*
19. Hawes, *Off Soundings*, 27.
20. Ibid., 26.
21. Ibid., 33.
22. Quoted in Jameson, *Privateering and Piracy*, 218.
23. Mayes thus began what would become known as the White Horse Tavern, the oldest operating tavern still in existence in New England.
24. Hawes, *Off Soundings*, 36.
25. Simmons, *Spirit of the New England Tribes*, 110–11.
26. Bridenbaugh, ed., *Gentlemen's Progress*, 151.
27. As quoted in Chapin's *Privateering in Rhode Island*, 55–58.
28. Munro, *Tales of an Old Sea Port*, 37.
29. For a detailed account of Defoe's influence on the adventure tale, see chapter two of Margaret Cohen's *The Novel and the Sea*, "Remarkable Occurrences at Sea and in the Novel," 59.
30. Paine, *Lost Ships and Lonely Seas*, 23–24.

Chapter 2

31. Stilgoe, *Lifeboat*, 53.
32. Coughtry, *The Notorious Triangle*, 56.
33. Bolster, *Black Jacks*, 78–79.
34. Emrich, *Folklore in the American Land*, 439.
35. Ibid., 438.
36. Ibid., 450.
37. Ibid., 455.
38. Ibid., 466.
39. Ibid., 468.
40. Snow, *Storms and Shipwrecks*, 204.
41. Barlow, *Journal*, 259.
42. Hamley, *History of Tattooing.*
43. From the journal of the *Yankee*, as printed in Munro, *Tales of an Old Sea Port*, 234–35.
44. From the journal of Francis Rogers, as printed in Rediker, *Between the Devil*, 187.

45. Olmstead, *Incidents of a Whaling Voyage*, 69–71.
46. This ancient superstition likely developed from the practice of casting ballast overboard preceding the event of a storm.
47. Rediker, *Between the Devil*, 180–81.
48. Dampier, *Dampier's New Voyage*, 295–96.
49. Eric Hanauer, "Seafaring Superstitions," http://www.dtmag.com.
50. Olmstead, *Incidents of a Whaling Voyage*.
51. Snow, *Marine Mysteries*, 213.

CHAPTER 3

52. Little, *Sea Rover's Practice*.
53. One amateur historian named Harry Knowles compiled a list of sixty-seven shipwrecks of official record between 1883 and 1952.
54. Gillis, *The Human Shore*, 102.
55. Letter from John Brown of Providence to his son James Brown of Philadelphia, November 17, 1782. Courtesy of Henry A.L. Brown.
56. Snow, *Storms and Shipwrecks*, 174.
57. Snow, *Marine Mysteries*, 53.
58. From the journal of the *Yankee*, as reprinted in Munro, *Tales of an Old Sea Port*, 230.
59. Olmstead, *Incidents of a Whaling Voyage*.
60. Ibid., 108.
61. Emerson is quoting Samuel Johnson's declaration of life at sea.
62. Emerson, "Journals," from *American Sea Writing*.
63. Journal of Captain William Driven, quoted in the *Essex County Chronicle*, May 25, 1999.
64. Chapin, *Rhode Island Privateers*, 130.
65. Hounds were projections at the masthead to support rigging, while bitts were posts on the deck for belaying purposes.
66. Referring to the gunwale.
67. Jameson, *Privateering and Piracy*, 406.
68. Gloucester Historical Archives, listings of those "Lost At Sea" with descriptions of circumstances, etc.
69. From Block Island Cemetery records, compiled and arranged by Helen Winslow, Mansfield, Rhode Island Historical Society, January 1954, p. 30.

70. Lost at Sea Register, City of Gloucester, Massachusetts. http://www.gloucester-ma.gov.

71. Ibid.

72. Thaxter, *Among the Isles of Shoals*, 62.

73. Little, *The Sea Rover's Practice*, 204.

74. Quoted from Barnstable neighbor Amis Otis in the notes to Downs's own memoir, *A Brief and Remarkable Narrative of the Life and Extreme Sufferings of Barnabas Downs Jun.*

75. Snow, *Storms and Shipwrecks*, 175.

76. Chapin, *Rhode Island Privateers*, 12. Howard Chapin wrote, "Crews of these privateers averaged more than 100 men."

77. Little, *The Sea Rover's Practice*, 98.

78. Ibid., 97.

79. Rediker, *The Amistad Rebellion*, 10.

80. Spears, *Story of the New England Whalers*, 363–64.

81. Hohman, *The American Whaleman*, 120.

82. Clipping of the *Boston Journal* in the Nicholson Collection, Providence Public Library, Series 1-R, Subseries 2, Folder 1.

83. Spears, *Story of the New England Whalers*, 289–92.

84. Olmstead, *Incidents of a Whaling Voyage*, 74–75.

85. Ibid., 25.

86. Ibid., 78.

87. Ibid., 98.

88. As reprinted in Ellis, *Monsters of the Sea*, 49.

89. Letter to Judge Davis from John Prince, Marshall of Massachusetts, August 16, 1818.

90. Sanford, *Scandalous Newport*, 39.

Chapter 4

91. Little, *The Sea Rover's Practice*, 205.

92. From the Nicholson Collection, Providence Public Library, E118, Box 1.

93. Little, *The Sea Rover's Practice*, 204.

94. Ibid.

95. Rediker, *Between the Devil*, 195.

96. Ibid., 197.

97. Ibid., 172–73.

98. Comer, "Diary," 66.

CHAPTER 5

99. Munro, *Tales from an Old Sea Port*, 284.

100. Broadsheet printed in Hartford in 1810. From the Hay Whaling Collection, Brown University.

101. Downs, *A Brief Narrative*.

102. Translation of *The Odyssey* by Robert Fitzgerald.

103. Gillis, *The Human Shore*, 140.

104. John Greenleaf Whittier, "The Palatine," *Atlantic Monthly*, July 1867.

105. This, the fourth stanza, is Whittier's only attempted translation of a Cape Cod accent, which translated to proper English would read: "Old Floyd Ireson, for his hard heart/Tarred and feathered and carried in a cart/By the women of Marblehead!"

106. "Shipwreck! Winslow Homer and the Lifeline," *Herald-Mail*, October 19, 2012.

CHAPTER 6

107. Spears, *New England Whalers*, 44.

108. Comer, "Diary," 47.

109. Mariners usually relate a "great sea" as the nineteenth-century definition of a large or "rogue" wave that swept the deck or even momentarily submerged the bow of the vessel.

110. Thoreau, *Cape Cod*, 21.

111. Thaxter, *Among the Isles of Shoals*. In Neill, *American Sea Writing*, 295.

112. Thaxter, *Among the Isles of Shoals*, 37–41.

113. Gleason, *Kindly Lights*.

114. Stedamn, "Point Judith Lighthouse," 7.

115. Letter from Captain Herbert Knowles to Horace Belcher, February 15, 1932. I am indebted to Henry A.L. Brown for this document.

116. Elisabeth Shure, "Whaler's Letters," Nantucket Historical Association. http://nha.org.

117. Ibid.

118. Ibid., from an article by Florence Mary Bennet, *Outlook Weekly*, September 10, 1924.

119. Ibid.

120. Diary of John R. Congdon, 1863, in the Congdon Family Papers, MSS Box 1, Folder 9, Rhode Island Historical Society.

121. Letter from A.C. Dickens to Henry R. Congdon, March 1863, in the Congdon Family Papers MSS 363 Box 3, Folder 27, Rhode Island Historical Society.

122. American Tract Society, Series 13, No. XXVII from the Hay Whaling Collection, Brown University, Providence, Rhode Island.

123. From the "Visitor's Guide to the Seaman's Bethel," New Bedford, Massachusetts.

Chapter 7

124. Bartlett, *Memoirs of Rhode Island Officers*.

125. Letter of Mary Elizabeth Hull, January 20, 2011.

Bibliography

Abbas, D.K. *Rhode Island in the Revolution: Big Happenings in the Smallest Colony*. Newport: Rhode Island Marine Archaeology Project, 2009.

Barlow, Edward. *Journal: Life At Sea (1659–1703)*. London: Hurst & Blackett, 1934.

Bartlett, John Russell. *Memoirs of Rhode Island Officers Who Were Engaged in the Service of Their Country During the Great Rebellion of the South, Illustrated with Thirty-Four Portraits*. Providence, RI: S.S. Rider and Brother, 1867.

Bolster, W. Jeffrey. *Black Jacks: African American Seamen in the Age of Sail*. Cambridge, MA: Harvard University Press, 1997.

Bridenbaugh, Carl. *Gentlemen's Progress: The Itinerarium of Dr. Alexander Hamilton, 1744*. Providence, RI: Brown University Press, 1948.

Carrol, Charles. "Journal." Unpublished, in the collection of the New Bedford Whaling Museum.

Chapin, Howard. *Rhode Island Privateers in King George's War, 1739–1748*. Providence: Rhode Island Historical Society, 1926.

Christopher, Emma. *Slave Ship Sailors and their Captive Cargoes, 1730–1807*. Cambridge: Cambridge University Press, 2007.

Cohen, Margaret. *The Novel and the Sea*. Princeton, NJ: Princeton University Press, 2010.

Comer, John. "Diary of John Comer." *Collections of the Rhode Island Historical Society* 8 (1893).

Congdon, John R. "Diary 1863." The Congdon Family Papers, MSS Box 1, Folder 9. Rhode Island Historical Society.

Coughtry, Jay. *The Notorious Triangle: Rhode Island and the African Slave Trade, 1700–1807*. Philadelphia, PA: Temple University Press, 1981.

Dampier, William. *Memoirs of a Buccaneer: Dampier's New Voyage Around the World 1697*. New York: Dover Maritime, 2007.

Downs, Barnabas. *A Brief and Remarkable Narrative of the Life and Extreme Sufferings of Barnabas Downs, Jun.* Boston: E. Russell, 1786.

Ellis, Peter. *Monsters of the Sea*. New York: Knopf, 1994.

Emerson, Ralph Waldo. "Journals." In *American Sea Writing*. Philbrick, ed. New York: Library of America, 2000.

Emrich, Duncan. *Folklore in the American Land*. Boston: Little, Brown and Company, 1972.

Gillis, John R. *The Human Shore*. Chicago: University of Chicago Press, 2012.

Gleason, Sarah C. *Kindly Lights: A History of the Lighthouses of Southern New England*. Boston: Beacon Press, 1991.

Hamley, W.D. *The History of Tattooing and Its Significance*. London: H.F. & G. Withorsby, 1925.

Hawes, Alexander Boyd. *Off Soundings: Aspects of the Maritime History of Rhode Island*. Chevy Chase, MD: Posterity Press, 1999.

Hitchings, Sinclair. "Guarding the New England Coast." In *Seafaring in Colonial Massachusetts*. Allis Jr., ed. Boston: Colonial Society of Massachusetts, 1980.

Hohman, Elmo Paul. *The American Whaleman: A Study of Life and Labor in the Whaling Industry*. New York: Longman, Green & Company, 1928.

Jameson, J. Franklin. *Privateering and Piracy in the Colonial Period*. New York: MacMillan Company, 1923.

Johnston, James C. *The Yankee Fleet*. Charleston, SC: The History Press, 2007.

Kurtz, Peter. *Bluejackets in the Blubber Room: A Biography of the* William Badger, *1828–1865*. Tuscaloosa: University of Alabama Press, 2013.

Linebaugh, Peter, and Marcus Rediker. *The Many-Headed Hydra: Sailors, Slaves, Commoners, and the Hidden History of the Revolutionary Atlantic*. Boston: Beacon Press, 2001.

Little, Benerson. *The Sea Rover's Practice: Pirate Tactics and Techniques, 1630–1730*. Washington, D.C.: Potomac Press, 2005.

Morison, Samuel Eliot. *The Maritime History of Massachusetts, 1783–1860*. Boston: Houghton Mifflin Company, 1941.

Munro, Wilfred Harold. *Tales of an Old Sea Port*. Princeton, NJ: Princeton University Press, 1917.

Olmstead, Francis Allen. *Incidents of a Whaling Voyage*. New York: D. Appleton & Company, 1841.

Paine, Ralph D. *Lost Ships and Lonely Seas.* New York: Century Company, 1921.

Rediker, Marcus. *The Amistad Rebellion.* New York: Viking, 2012.

———. *Between the Devil and the Deep Blue Sea: Merchant Seamen, Pirates, and the Anglo-Saxon Maritime World, 1700–1750.* Cambridge: Cambridge University Press, 1987.

Sanford, Larry. *Scandalous Newport.* Charleston, SC: The History Press, 2013.

Simmons, William S. *Spirit of the New England Tribes: Indian History and Folklore, 1620–1984.* Hanover, NH: University Press of New England, 1986.

Snow, Edward Rowe. *Marine Mysteries and Dramatic Disasters of New England.* New York: Dodd, Mead & Company, 1976.

———. *Storms and Shipwrecks of New England.* Carlisle, MA: Commonwealth Editions, 2003.

Spears, John R. *The Story of the New England Whalers.* New York: MacMillan Company, 1922.

Stedamn, Oliver R. "Point Judith Lighthouse." From *Ships, Sailors, and Seaports.* Kingston, RI: Pettaquamscutt Historical Society, 1963.

Stilgoe, John R. *Lifeboat: A History of Courage, Cravenness, and Survival at Sea.* Charlottesville: University of Virginia Press, 2003.

Thaxter, Cecelia. *Among the Isles of Shoals.* New York: Houghton, Mifflin and Company, 1899.

Thoreau, Henry David. *Cape Cod.* Boston: Norton and Co., ed., 1951.

Vietze, Andrew, and Stephen Erickson. *Boon Island: A True Story of Mutiny, Shipwreck, and Cannibalism.* Guilford, CT: Globe Pequot Press, 2012.

Wroth, Henry. *The Way of a Ship.* Providence, RI: John Carter Brown Library, 2011.

Index

About the Author

R obert A. Geake is the author of four previously published books of local history, including *A History of the Providence River* and *Historic Taverns of Rhode Island,* both from The History Press. His blog on New England history can be found at http://www.rifootprints.com.